REEXAMINING
READING DIAGNOSIS

New Trends and Procedures

Susan Mandel Glazer
Rider College

Lyndon W. Searfoss
Arizona State University

Lance M. Gentile
University of North Carolina at Asheville

Editors

89-959

ira

International Reading Association
Newark, Delaware 19714

INTERNATIONAL READING ASSOCIATION

Copyright 1988 by the
International Reading Association, Inc.

Library of Congress Cataloging in Publication Data

Reexamining reading diagnosis.
     Includes bibliographies.
     1. Reading—Ability testing—Evaluation. I. Glazer,
Susan Mandel.   II. Searfoss, Lyndon W.   III. Gentile, Lance M.   IV.
Title: Reexamining reading diagnosis.
LB1050.46.R43   1988   428.4'076   88-3030
ISBN 0-87207-532-X

Cover design by Boni Nash

Contents

Foreword

T his book is a revelation to one who has been active in the field of diagnosis and remediation of reading disabilities for more than thirty years. The contributors suggest dozens of informal steps of observation techniques, schemes for charting and outlining, sampling recall or retelling, and other ways of analyzing children's reading. Each analytic effort is matched with appropriate remedial instruction steps. Even the familiar clinical or psychometric approach is represented. No educational level is omitted in the continuum of informal diagnostic efforts.

These approaches to understanding children's reading behaviors are in effect naturalistic assessments in multiple settings. They are a sharp contrast to the common practice of using commercial tests. Teachers function as observers, recorders, providers of outlines or charts, and frequently as interactants while students demonstrate their knowledge of text structure, pursue a think aloud protocol, or complete a structural or graphic organizer. In their description of these techniques and the relevant instructional practices, the contributors to *Reexamining Reading Diagnosis: New Trends and Procedures* have provided a model that both teachers and teacher training institutions should incorporate in their efforts.

George D. Spache

Preface

T he authors of this volume have contributed their knowledge to IRA members in two preconvention institutes that were concerned with new trends in diagnostic procedures for classrooms and clinics. The success of those institutes was the impetus for this monograph. We have used the strengths of each contributor to create a diverse, up to date text offering teachers in classrooms and clinics new diagnostic procedures and ideas based on current theoretical and pedagogical trends.

SMG
LWS
LMG

Contributors

Jules C. Abrams
Hahnemann University
Philadelphia, Pennsylvania

Thomas W. Bean
California State University
Fullerton, California

Carol S. Brown
Rider College
Lawrenceville, New Jersey

Margaret A. Cagney
Glassboro State College
Glassboro, New Jersey

Maryann Eeds
Arizona State University
Tempe, Arizona

Lance M. Gentile
University of North Carolina
Asheville, North Carolina

Susan Mandel Glazer
Rider College
Lawrenceville, New Jersey

Susan L. Lytle
University of Pennsylvania
Philadelphia, Pennsylvania

Michael A. Martin
Eastern Michigan University
Ypsilanti, Michigan

Merna M. McMillan
Santa Barbara Health Care Services/
Mental Health
Santa Barbara, California

Lesley Mandel Morrow
Rutgers University
New Brunswick, New Jersey

John E. Readence
Louisiana State University
Baton Rouge, Louisiana

Lyndon W. Searfoss
Arizona State University
Tempe, Arizona

Albert J. Shannon
St. Joseph's University
Philadelphia, Pennsylvania

Gloria B. Smith
Rider College
Lawrenceville, New Jersey

Susan Mandel Glazer
Lyndon W. Searfoss

1

Reexamining Reading Diagnosis

W hy reexamine reading diagnosis? Because it is time. It is time because definitions of the reading process and purposes for instruction have changed, classroom and clinical pedagogical procedures have changed, and the population of students and our expectations about literacy for these students have changed. We will discuss these issues as described in the accompanying graphic organizer.

How Definitions of the Reading Process Have Changed

Definitions of reading over the past century have come full circle. We have moved from defining reading as process to defining it as a product and back again to a process. Current research demonstrates that reading involves strategies that force us to go beyond the printed page (Collins, Brown, & Larkin, 1980; Tierney & Pearson, 1983).

Explanations of the reading process reflect social, political, and cultural pressures. All of us who have contributed to this volume would like to think we have created original ideas and tools to assess reading. Actually, we are haunted by the works of theorists of the past whose ideas are strikingly similar to our own.

The story of American reading instruction, told by Nila Banton Smith (1965), reflects society's attempt to apply science to education. A look at several definitions of reading, beginning with Huey (1908, 1968), demonstrates this. Huey (1968, p. 1) wrote,

1

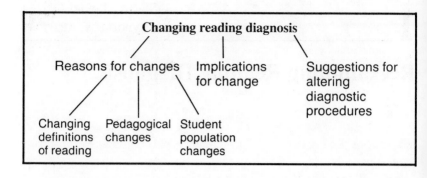

Changing reading diagnosis

Reasons for changes — Implications for change — Suggestions for altering diagnostic procedures

Changing definitions of reading — Pedagogical changes — Student population changes

Reading, for our Anglo-Saxon forefathers, meant counseling or advising oneself or others (A.-S. *radan,* to advise). To read was to get or to give counsel from a book, originally from a piece of bark on which characters were inscribed, at least if the reputed connection of *book* and *beech* can be sustained. The accessory notion of talking aloud seems to have been implied in the word, as it was also in the Roman word for reading. To the Roman, on the other hand, reading meant gathering or choosing (*lectio,* reading, from *lego,* to gather) from what was written, suggesting that constant feeling of values which goes on in all effective reading.

Based on our current interest in prior knowledge and prediction, we believe Huey's interest in studies of perception and its relationship to the reading process was insightful (Javel, 1879, Cattell, 1886, cited in Huey, 1968). Huey was concerned with the processes used to gain information from the printed page. He focused particularly on the ideas represented in printed form and the means by which the mind takes note of them. He believed that reading was an activity that went beyond the eye.

Thorndike (1917, pp. 323-332) defined reading as thinking and assumed that it was a process. He wrote,

> Reading is a very elaborate procedure, involving a weighing of each of the many elements in a sentence, their organization in proper relations to one another, the selection of certain of their connotations and the rejection of others, and the

cooperation of many forces to determine final response . . . . Understanding a paragraph is like solving a problem in mathematics. It consists in selecting the right elements of the situation and putting them together in the right relations, and also with the right amount of weight or influence or force for each.

Huey's and Thorndike's ideas are predecessors of current models that describe reading as more than the interpretation of orthographic symbols. Their definitions and explanations reflect the belief that reading requires both visual and nonvisual information. They support recent findings that prior knowledge about an experience involving language—the syntactic, semantic, and orthographic elements used to create text—is stored in readers' minds, enabling them to predict meaning.

Careful reading of Huey and Thorndike reveals that today's definitions of reading are expanded but not substantially different. Current scholars have elaborated on Huey's and Thorndike's notions to include all forms and elements of communication used interactively by human beings to solve problems during reading and related activities (Goodman, 1967; Just & Carpenter, 1987; Rumelhart, 1985; Tierney & Pearson, 1983; Valencia & Pearson, 1987). The expanded notion includes oral language (listening and speaking), writing, body language (kinetics), and thinking. The reader must use all of these effectively for successful text comprehension. Students also must learn more than what Yetta Goodman refers to as "school reading skills." In informal conversation, Goodman has referred to such skills as those useful to children only for proving they can pass reading tests. Levine (1982) concurs with Goodman and insists that definitions of reading be expanded so they might be considered definitions of literacy. His notion that there are "massive differences between school literacy, which largely consists of academic exercises imposed on pupils as a curricular end in itself, and adult literacy, whose instrumental character naturally derives from its capacity to serve adult needs and projects" (p. 262) must be accepted for diagnostic as well as pedagogical purposes.

We believe that definitions of reading applied to diagnostic procedures have been limited and confined to school reading skills.

We also believe that constrained measuring techniques have been used for so long because they are "manageable." Measuring the interactive relationships among the syntactic, semantic, and orthographic elements of reading, writing, oral language, and body language presents overwhelming challenges to professionals. Developing instructional environments for guiding students to use language interactively has been easier, just as it has been easier to move from the mastery learning of the 1960s to today's practices of matching students with appropriate methods and materials (Valencia & Pearson, 1987). Our goals in this text focus on changes in assessment procedures that reflect today's instructional practices.

How Pedagogy Has Changed in Classrooms and Clinics

Instruction in reading has begun to move from teacher directed to student directed activities, from moving students through skill development worksheets to guiding them to understanding the processes and strategies they need to use to comprehend text. What has taken place is a shift of power. In the past, teachers have assumed the responsibility for children's learning. This assumption, which provides teachers with the power to teach their students, assumes that teachers can teach students to learn specific concepts, ideas, and activities, while denying students the power to communicate. For students to become empowered, they must understand how they create meaning through various forms of communication. This ability, which focuses on knowing which strategies to use to accomplish goals, provides students with the power to manipulate their ideas in conventional formats for sharing. Empowered students realize that the knowledge and purpose they bring to the text is as important as, or even more important than, the text information itself. These notions, supported by current research (Anderson et al., 1976; Anderson, Spiro, & Anderson, 1977; Rumelhart, 1981), demonstrate that classroom applications that guide students to tap prior knowledge about content and structure of reading materials provide a means for comprehending text effectively (Hansen & Pearson, 1982; Meyer, 1984). This focus has resulted in more student centered instruction. A comparison of the foci of traditional and current notions about literacy learning as summarized by Glazer and Searfoss (1988) follows.

Traditional Notions	Changes in Notions
Emphasis is on making meaning from graphic symbols and on word identification.	Emphasis is on thought processes and language competence. Thought and language play interactive roles when constructing meaning from text.
Instructional procedures go from letter learning to words to sentences. Lessons proceed from parts and move to wholes. Ideas move from specifics to generalizations.	Students begin with whole units—stories, poems, etc.—and move from generalizations to specifics.
Comprehension is viewed as a product that results from a student's ability to call words and offer expected answers to questions and assignments.	Comprehension is viewed as a process. Students use language cues to search their memories to predict outcomes. Stimuli generate acceptable responses. Each student's perceptions of ideas, text, etc. are respected.
Reading instruction is viewed as strategies to guide students to translate graphic symbols into oral language.	In reading instruction, ideas are more important than printed words.
Written language is subservient to oral language behaviors.	As the reader becomes skilled, graphic information is less important. Clues for meaning from readers' perceptions take precedence.

How Student Populations and Expectations Have Changed

Student populations have increased and changed dramatically since the end of World War II. Mandatory school enrollment laws require children from all cultures and all socioeconomic and political groups to attend the same schools. Children from poor and illiterate homes join those from homes where the processes of education and reading are part of children's natural development. We in the United States have believed in this process of natural development since Jean Jacques Rousseau applied the principles of natural growth to French children in the eighteenth century. Rousseau's thoughts concurred with the American educational philosopher Dewey, who also believed that a child's intellectual and social skills would develop naturally through experiences in an active environment.

Despite these ideas, most school curricula are prescribed. Educators who espouse these prescriptive curricula (beginning with Plato) believe that letting children grow naturally does not provide them with sufficient information to survive in a literate society.

Hirsch (1987) suggests that there is an essential knowledge base necessary for literacy. He refers to those who possess this base as "cultural literates," a term Hirsch defines as coinciding with Chall's "world knowledge" concept. Cultural literacy consists of a "network of information that all competent readers possess (p. 2). Using this knowledge probably means scoring adequately on standardized tests. The larger issue deals with what knowledge is necessary to be considered culturally literate both in and out of school, since that knowledge makes learning to read possible (Thorndike, 1973).

Although children learn to be literate at home, they are expected to learn literacy skills in schools. Children from varied backgrounds who come to these institutions incorporate individual schemata from home environments that control student's expectations, beliefs, and the responses they offer as they solve problems in school. Youngsters develop expectations about school behavior, about elements of language and how to use them, and about ways to solve problems. The knowledge that helps them "read" their worlds

Glazer and Searfoss

in order to maintain some level of control is learned before they get to school. When there are problems in school and schemata for solving them exist in students' minds, success is likely. When school problems arise and students' expectations and schemata for dealing with them are drastically different from those they've learned in early years, failures result.

The Diagnostic Implications

Our discussion seems important when reviewing most current assessment procedures. Testing by prescription means prescriptive curricula. If we believe in the uniqueness of individuals, prescriptive curricula and tests to assess the effectiveness of these curricula seem inappropriate.

Our populations and expectations for students and teachers have changed, and our definitions of literacy processes have expanded. Our pedagogy has expanded to reflect current research about learning literacy skills. Our tests and testing environments, however, have changed little. The testing mentality of our society perpetuates itself and remains rigid. Hirsch's notion is timely, since the public seems to want to hear that there is a body of knowledge that creates literate students. We wish that were so; then we would have literate students who could employ literacy skills for success both in school and out. When diagnosing students' abilities, we would be able to follow traditional notions about learning to read. Diagnostic procedures could determine "levels of knowleldge" for grade placement. If students were found to have deficits, we could label them (learning disabled, dyslexic) and place them in special classes. Actions taken as a result of this one test session (or score) criterion could be prescriptive and definitive, since the assessment procedures were conducted by prescription.

Although we have learned that prior knowledge and the ability to predict what is in reading materials greatly influence comprehension, tests do not consider these elements. Tests provide few occasions for students to use their perceptions of ideas to create or choose questions about what they read. We know of no standardized testing tool that assesses the strategies students use for learning.

There are few instruments that use complete stories, poems, or content passages.

As we have considered current expectations, we marvel at how well students have responded, considering the impediments under which they are expected to function. The environments in which students take tests are appalling. They seldom resemble the instructional setting in which students learn to read.

How We Can Create Better Assessment Situations

Assessment procedures and their purposes must be redirected to assess students' strengths instead of deficits. This idea is not new. Students should be *observed* in activities where successful text comprehension occurs. This requires expanding the places where we assess students. The diagnostic process must include observing students interacting with effective teaching methods and learning materials. Such diagnostic procedures require continuous observation over time in many settings. This naturalistic approach to assessment views the learner during the learning process, recognizing the social, political, and cultural diversities among students. It demands that students learn from one another and teachers learn from students; it demands that environments include humor, since learning is often tedious, difficult, and frustrating.

Learning to observe reading behaviors in varied settings demands concentration and trial and error. The activities involved might be compared to reading a complicated passage of text. You must encode the complicated text by reconstructing meanings for yourself. In order to construct meanings about student behavior, you must learn how to observe students' approaches to constructing meaning, which requires an element of expertise unnecessary in traditional testing. The observer must note growth and changes, then record the data and interpret its meanings. Astute watchers develop questions as they observe students in reading, writing, listening, and other language behaviors. After a period of observation, appropriate pedagogical goals might be developed, based on tentative conclusions considering each student's strengths and needs.

Researchers and theorists (Johnston, 1987; Paratore & Indrisano, 1987) are developing realistic models of assessment. Our model, C-A-L-M (a suitable anachronism for the teacher/researcher who diagnoses in classrooms and clinics), represents one way of describing a naturalistic approach to assessment. It eliminates the notion of one testing session, thus eliminating stress, since there are many chances to observe the performance of students and teachers. The Cumulative Assessment of Language Model (Glazer & Searfoss, 1988) in the Figure provides one framework for using multiple tools, multiple environments, multiple strategies, and multiple settings for collecting data on which to base descriptions of students' performances in reading.

Continuous Assessment of Language
Model: CALM

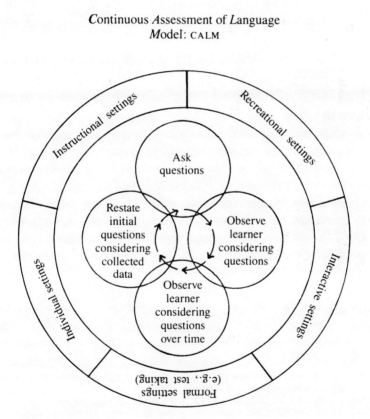

From Susan Mandel Glazer and Lyndon W. Searfoss. *Reading diagnosis and instruction: A C-A-L-M approach.* Englewood Cliffs, NJ: Prentice-Hall, 1988. Used with permission.

The model also demands that teachers evaluate themselves during the assessment process by asking themselves the following questions.

1. Am I observing students reading in
   recreational settings?
   instructional settings?
   interactive settings?
   individual (tutorial) settings?
   formal test taking settings?
2. Have I collected sufficient data about the students as they interact with text materials in these settings to make appropriate pedagogical changes?
3. Have I collected the data considering my question about the behavior?
4. Was my question appropriate? What do I observe (ask) next?

Summary

Realistic evaluation means evaluating students and ourselves. Self-evaluation encourages students to continually look at themselves. Repeatedly asking questions about self, our instructional effectiveness, and our abilities to change helps us serve as models for students doing the same. Evaluation, in the global sense, demands that we review how we think about ideas to create and respond to various tests. Once we know the "how" about our learning, we can make effective changes in ourselves and in our teaching procedures, thus positively affecting students' literate lives.

References

Anderson, R.C., Reynolds, R.E., Schallert, D.L., and Goetz, E.T. *Frameworks for comprehending discourse.* Report No. 12. Champaign, IL: Center for the Study of Reading, University of Illinois, 1976.

Anderson, R.C., Spiro, R.J., and Anderson, M.C. *Schemata as scaffolding for the representation of information in connected discourse.* Report No. 24. Champaign, IL: Center for the Study of Reading, University of Illinois, 1977.

Collins, A., Brown, J.S., and Larkin, K.M. Inferences in text understanding. In R.J. Spiro, B.C. Bruce, and W.F. Brewer (Eds.), *Theoretical issues in reading comprehension.* Hillsdale, NJ: Erlbaum, 1980.

Glazer, S.M., and Searfoss, L.W. *Reading diagnosis and instruction: A C-A-L-M approach.* Englewood Cliffs, NJ: Prentice-Hall, 1988.

Goodman, K.S. Reading: A psycholinguistic guessing game. In H. Singer and R.B. Ruddell (Eds.), *Theoretical models and processes of reading*. Newark, DE: International Reading Association, 1970, 259-272.

Hansen, J., and Pearson, P.D. *An instructional study: Improving the inferential comprehension of good and poor fourth grade readers*. Report No. 235. Champaign, IL: Center for the Study of Reading, University of Illinois, 1982.

Hirsch, E.D., Jr. *Cultural literacy*. Boston: Houghton-Mifflin, 1987.

Huey, E.B. *The psychology and pedagogy of reading*. New York: MIT Press, 1968. (Original work published 1908.)

Johnston, P. Steps toward a more naturalistic approach to the assessment of the reading process. In J. Algina (Ed.), *Advances in content based educational assessment*. Norwood, NJ: Ablex, 1987.

Just, M.A., and Carpenter, P.A. *The psychology of reading and language comprehension*. Newton, MA: Allyn and Bacon, 1987.

Levine, K. Functional literacy: Fond illusions and false economics. *Harvard Educational Review*, 1982, *52*, 249-266.

Meyer, B. Organizational aspects of texts: Effects on reading comprehension and application for classroom. In J. Flood (Ed.), *Promoting reading comprehension*. Newark, DE: International Reading Association, 1984, 113-138.

Paratore, J.R., and Indrisano, R. Intervention assessment in reading comprehension. *The Reading Teacher*, 1987, *40* (8), 778-783.

Rumelhart, D. Schemata: The building blocks of cognition. In J.T. Guthrie (Ed.), *Comprehension and teaching*. Newark, DE: International Reading Association, 1981, 3-26.

Rumelhart, D.E. Toward an interactive model of reading. In H. Singer and R.B. Ruddell (Eds.), *Theoretical models and processes of reading*, third edition. Newark, DE: International Reading Association, 1985, 722-750.

Smith, N.B. *American reading instruction*. Newark, DE: International Reading Association, 1986.

Tierney, R.J., and Pearson, P.D. Toward a composing model of reading. *Language Arts*, 1983, *60* (5), 568-580.

Thorndike, E.L. Reading as reasoning: A study of mistakes in paragraph reading. *Journal of Educational Psychology*, 1917, *8* (6) 323-332.

Thorndike, R.L. *Reading comprehension education in fifteen countries: An empirical study*. New York: John Wiley & Sons, 1973.

Valencia, S., and Pearson, P.D. Reading assessment: Time for a change. *The Reading Teacher*, 1987, *40* (8), 726-732.

Lance M. Gentile
Merna M. McMillan

2

Reexamining the Role of Emotional Maladjustment*

T he purposes and goals of this chapter are fourfold: (1) To present research findings related to emotional maladjustment and reading, (2) to consider stress as a significant factor in emotional maladjustment to reading, (3) to provide an instrument that may assist in identifying specific stress reactions to reading, and (4) to suggest effective approaches for working with students whose maladjustment to reading may be either the source or result of their emotional difficulties.

The accompanying graphic organizer provides the structure for this chapter.

Research

Many studies suggest students with reading difficulties demonstrate behavior associated with emotional maladjustment at home, at school, or both (Dolch, 1931, 1951; Robinson, 1946, 1964; Spache, 1976). Moreover, the literature points to a strong connection between stress and reading difficulties (Gentile, McMillan, & Swain, 1985). These studies also indicate that when students experience emotional trauma during reading, they often are unwilling or unable to concentrate (Allington, 1980; Blanchard, 1936; Gann, 1945; Gates, 1941; Natchez, 1959). Under these circumstances, reading may evoke specific maladaptive stress reactions that inhibit students' learning (Cannon, 1915; Selye, 1956,

*Adapted from Lance M. Gentile and Merna M. McMillan, *Stress and reading difficulties: Research, assessment, intervention.* Newark, DE: International Reading Association, 1987.

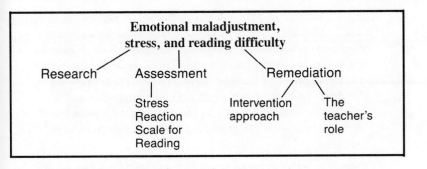

Emotional maladjustment, stress, and reading difficulty

Research — Assessment — Remediation

Assessment:
Stress Reaction Scale for Reading

Remediation:
Intervention approach

The teacher's role

1976; Weinberg & Rehmet, 1983). These reactions have been found to be both physical and psychological and are manifested in a range of behavior from anger and aggression [fight] to avoidance and apprehension [flight] (Bird, 1927; Dreikurs, 1954, 1964; Freud, 1935; Wiskell, 1948). Finally, some studies and theories show that, overtly or covertly, parents, teachers, or peers may contribute to making reading threatening or stressful (Deci, 1985; McDermott, 1977; Silverman, Fite, & Mosher, 1959).

Assessment

To date, most efforts to measure and remediate reading difficulties are based on standardized or informal skills tests. Underlying these tests is the notion that if teachers can identify specific skills deficits, they will be able to find an instructional cure to relieve the symptoms of reading difficulty. This reductionist view of reading may contribute to the fact that research fails to show many long term gains or lasting effects of remedial reading instruction. Johnston (1985, pp. 174-175) noted,

> Past attempts at explanations of the differences between good and poor readers have tended to dwell on the minutiae of mental operations without considering either the psychological or social contexts in which they occur . . . . Most current explanations of reading difficulties focus on the level of operations, devoid of context, goals, motives or history. While some work has focused on the context of read-

ing failure rather than mental operations (McDermott, 1977; Mehan, 1979), there has been little effort to integrate these two dimensions. The consequent explanations of reading failure are sterile and have resulted in more or less terminal diagnoses of reading failure. Until we can integrate the depth of human feeling and thinking into our understanding of reading difficulties, we will have only a shadow of an explanation of the problem and ill-directed attempts at solutions.

One reason most remedial reading programs focus only on skills deficits is that school administrators and state legislators use only the results of standardized reading skills tests for determining good and poor readers, comparing schools, and judging teacher effectiveness. While these tests may be a useful measure for comparing students within or among groups, they should not be used as the sole basis for designing remediation in reading. According to Moffett (1985, p. 52), "If it's not tested, it's not taught."

Assessment and intervention must go beyond skills deficits and consider the following points:

- It is as important to understand, measure, and address the social and emotional variables that form the core of many students' struggles or failures in reading as it is to test and evaluate their basic reading skills deficits. Relying solely on skills deficits to identify students' difficulties in reading is inadequate for helping them learn to read and make a better adjustment to reading.
- The whole of reading is greater than the sum of the parts. Undeniably, skills are important in reading, as is time on task skills practice, but social and emotional adjustments determine how little or how much a student brings to and derives from reading and reading instruction (Dreikurs, 1954; Gentile & McMillan, 1981).
- Many students with reading difficulties can demonstrate some level of skills mastery compared with other students of the same age or grade level (Lamb, 1985), but standardized test results fail to show what students are capable of doing. In most cases, skills test results reveal the approxi-

Gentile and McMillan

mate level at which a student's growth in reading stops. Missing from these test results are two important pieces of information relevant to helping students learn to cope effectively with reading difficulty: How hard did students try? What coping skills did they demonstrate when the test became difficult? (Gentile, McMillan, & Swain, 1985).

Students' perceptions of their testing and reading capabilities affect what they choose to do, how much effort they mobilize, how long they persevere in the face of difficulties, their thought patterns, and the amount of stress they experience in taxing situations.

Successful readers respond flexibly to the emotional challenges of tests and reading assignments. They perceive reading as challenging not threatening; they anticipate positive results for their efforts. Consequently, they have developed reading skills and study habits that permit them to work effectively, to assume responsibility for their own learning, to be comfortable and relaxed while reading, and to resolve their own difficulties.

In general, most successful readers are accepted by their peers. They are supported and encouraged by parents and teachers who expect them to succeed. Usually they are friendly, polite, and cooperative. They read independently, concentrate, and complete assignments satisfactorily and on time. While they may experience some difficulty or make mistakes in reading, they cope effectively and show steady improvement. They have learned to overcome problems through diligence; patience; and focused, consistent effort. They recognize their limitations yet work to strengthen their reading.

However, poor readers face many problems in addition to their skills deficits. Silverman, Fite, and Mosher (1959, p. 299) said, "Considering reading difficulties as a symptom, if all efforts then are aimed at curing the specific symptom, we might expect these efforts to be of no more avail than painting away the spots to cure the measles." Of greater significance are students' reactions to reading when it is stressful for them because these responses have the capacity to dictate and disrupt all future experience with written matter (Laurita, 1985).

Poor readers perceive reading as a threat and frequently exhibit maladaptive stress reactions when they read. Poor readers also display self-deprecation, lack of a clear system of goals or values, vulnerability to disparagment by others, immature relationships with parents or teachers, lack of insight into personal problems, or a pervasive depression (Maxwell, 1971).

Other researchers have provided detailed descriptions of students' maladaptive stress reactions to reading. Gentile and McMillan (1984) and Swain (1985) analyzed the records of 500 students with reading difficulties referred to an interdisciplinary, diagnostic, and remedial center over a seven year period. All the students were given a full multidisciplinary assessment; none was diagnosed as having neurological, psychological, or other physical impairments that would alter the expectation of normal development in reading. Data were drawn from referral and evaluation statements of parents, teachers, reading specialists, and counselors; observational information recorded during the administration of formal and informal tests; and statements gleaned from diagnostic or prescriptive reports. The descriptions were consolidated and classified. What emerged was a spectrum of fight or flight behavioral categories ranging from hostility and rage to immobilization and retreat.

From these studies Gentile and McMillan (1984) developed the Stress Reaction Scale for Reading. This scale can be used to identify students' maladaptive, fight or flight stress reactions to reading and to guide the use of appropriate instructional techniques. The instrument is designed to provide an overall impression of students' reactions to reading. Because of the complexity of reading problems, these emotional reactions are difficult to categorize precisely. Rather, the Scale is intended to show behavior trends when reading is stressful. The scale is not all inclusive and should be used only as an observational tool.

Stress Reaction Scale for Reading
For each of the following phrases, circle the letter, *a* or *b*, that most accurately describes the student's reactions when asked to read or during reading. If *neither one* applies write *N/O* on the blank to the right of each pair.

When asked to read or during reading, this student:

1. a. exhibits overt hostility or rage.
   b. becomes anxious or apprehensive. _____

2. a. becomes sullen or exhibits aggressive, acting out behavior.
   b. appears indifferent, insecure, or fearful. _____

3. a. responds impulsively to requests or questions, blurts out answers and offers information that is irrelevant or inaccurate.
   b. appears subdued, overly withdrawn, and depressed. _____

4. a. throws temper tantrums, cries, or becomes verbally abusive.
   b. seeks an escape or runs and hides. _____

5. a. clenches fists, becomes rigid, defiant, and angry.
   b. appears despondent, passive, and unable to concentrate. _____

6. a. becomes defensive and resistive, verbalizes or expresses an attitude of "I don't want to."
   b. lacks confidence, appears timid, verbalizes or expresses an attitude of "I can't, it's too hard." _____

7. a. demands entertaining, easy, or expedient activities, shows no tolerance for difficulty or challenge.
   b. takes no risks in challenging situations, constantly answers, "I don't know," even when answers are obvious. _____

8. a. refuses to comply, does not follow directions or complete assignments.
   b. appears embarrassed, daydreams, or frets over lack of ability. _____

9. a. becomes upset with change in routine, manipulates the situation to satisfy personal needs or whims.
   b. requires constant assurance, frequently checks with teacher by asking, "Did I get that right?" or "Was that good?" _____

10. a. seeks to disrupt the teacher, the lesson, or other students.
    b. expresses fear of rejection by parents, teachers, or peers for reading weaknesses. _____

11. a. uses any excuse for not being able to participate, temporizes until parent or teacher gives up.
    b. skips over material, ignores punctuation, inserts or deletes words and phrases, unable to follow structure or order. _____

12. a. demands constant supervision, attention, or guidance, refuses to do any independent reading.
    b. will try as long as parent or teacher closely monitors situation, appears helpless when left to work independently. _____

13. a. provides sarcastic, bizarre, or nonsensical answers to teachers' questions; makes weird sounds; sings; or bursts into loud, raucous laughter.
    b. becomes excessively self-critical, says things like, "I'm dumb," "I never get anything right," or "I'm not a good reader." _____

14. a. declares reading is "boring," "no fun," "hard work," refuses to cooperate.
    b. tries too hard, is immobolized by perceived failure. _____

15. a. makes little or no effort to succeed; shows disdain for activities; voices anger or displeasure at parents, teachers, and students who offer assistance.
    b. verbalizes or expresses an attitude of apathy, shows no willingness to try. _____

Interpreting the Stress Reaction Scale for Reading

To determine the *fight* reactions, count and record the number of *a*'s circled. For the *flight* reactions, count the number of *b*'s. Typically, one pattern will dominate. It is not unusual for a student to have some *a*'s and some *b*'s circled or to have some *N/O*'s recorded. A combination of interventional methods and materials is needed where a pattern is not consistent.

Remediation

When reading is stressful, students often try to avoid or escape the source of their discomfort. Fight or flight reactions tend to reinforce themselves because they reduce stress or anxiety. Therefore, such reactions are difficult to change.

After a student's pattern of responses to reading is determined, the next step is to plan appropriate intervention and to direct the role played by the teacher in remediation. When working with students who demonstrate a fight or flight response, the teacher

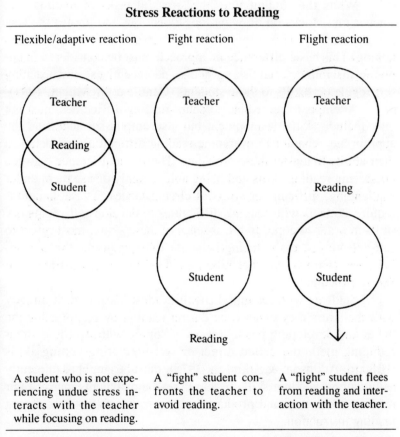

Stress Reactions to Reading

Flexible/adaptive reaction	Fight reaction	Flight reaction
A student who is not experiencing undue stress interacts with the teacher while focusing on reading.	A "fight" student confronts the teacher to avoid reading.	A "flight" student flees from reading and interaction with the teacher.

From Lance M. Gentile and Merna M. McMillan, *Stress and reading difficulties: Research, assessment, intervention.* Copyright 1987 by the International Reading Association.

must understand the types of interactions that may take place between student and teacher. The Figure illustrates this principle.

The adaptive reaction shows an integrated relationship between the teacher and student around reading. The fight reaction shows the student avoiding reading by confronting the teacher and leaving the assignment behind. The flight reaction shows the student escaping from reading and the teacher. For the student who demonstrates a fight reaction, a strategy must be designed to move the student away from the confrontation or "fight" with the teacher and back to the reading assignment. This requires a concise and consistent approach with a minimum of verbal interaction and prompting.

When the student flees the stressful tasks of reading, the teacher must focus on drawing the student out and toward the task and the teacher. This requires direct intervention, prompting, and talking. This basic difference in approach must be considered in applying discipline, establishing goals and incentives, and teaching self-regulatory skills to these students (Gentile & McMillan, 1987).

Attempts to remediate students' reading difficulties must not only include skills development but also emphasize acquiring the appropriate behavior to overcome reading difficulties and belief in their ability to master these problems. There is a difference between possessing reading skills and being able to apply or use them under challenging, difficult, or stressful circumstances. These situations require students with reading difficulties to develop self-regulatory skills in order to cope. In the absence of these skills, most resort to self-defeating stress-reducing behavior to expunge the threat reading poses to them, whether it be loss of self-esteem, frustration, or fear of ridicule.

Students with reading difficulties must learn to deal directly with the stress they experience during reading by reappraising the threat and developing positive ways of coping with it. These stress reducing methods, called direct or self-regulating coping skills (Hilgard, Atkinson, & Atkinson, 1975), must be taught as diligently as functional reading skills because they help students master their reading difficulties and produce long term, positive effects during reading instruction.

The two main features of teaching direct coping methods to students with reading difficulties are the interventional approach and the role of the teacher.

The Intervention Approach

Remedial reading programs are bolstered when students are taught three major coping or self-regulatory skills: goal setting, self-incentives, and self-monitoring (Bandura, 1977; Kanfer, 1980; Runck, 1982).

Goal Setting. White (1959) posited that humans have a basic, lifelong drive for ordering and mastering the environment. This drive is so strong that when order does not exist, a person will tend to impose order on external phenomena (the parallel for internal phenomena would be self-consistency). Ordering the environment reduces the uncertainty about what to expect, giving the individual better powers of prediction and control and, hence, reinforcing feelings of security by reducing the anxiety associated with uncertainty.

Teachers can help students regulate their reading difficulties by establishing explicit, reasonable, and reachable goals. Getting students to make self-directed changes in their reading requires the development of standards and goals to motivate and guide them. Bandura (1985, p. 9) described this process:

> When people commit themselves to explicit goals, negative discrepancies between what they do and what they seek to achieve serve as motivators for change. By making self-satisfaction contingent on goal attainment, people persist in their efforts until their attainments match what they are seeking to achieve.

The purpose of many reading assignments may be unclear and meaningless to students with reading difficulties. These students do not understand that what they are doing will help them become better readers and improve their chances of succeeding in school. Reading assignments seem unrelated to their goals and provide no assistance in overcoming their educational or personal problems. In fact, these assignments may only highlight perceived incompetencies. Teachers can aid students with reading difficulties by helping them establish explicit goals and by providing performance feedback.

Whether students with reading difficulties are motivated or discouraged when they fail to attain goals they have set for themselves is ultimately determined by their perceptions of their capacity to attain the goal. According to Bandura (1985, p. 10), "Those who doubt their capabilities are easily discouraged by failure, whereas those who are highly assured of their efficacy for goal attainment intensify their efforts when their attainments fall short, and persevere until they succeed."

Research has shown goal setting along with performance feedback to be highly effective in developing self-motivation (Locke et al., 1981). The degree to which establishing goals is an incentive for self-directed change in reading is dependent on three things:

1. The explicitness of the goals. Explicit goals provide clear guides for action as well as the means for students and teachers to evaluate performance. General goals are too vague and fail to direct students' motivation and behavior in reading instruction.
2. The level of the goals. Setting reasonable goals, working through incremental instructional steps, and making constructive appraisals of achievement sustain students' motivation and self-directed changes in reading. Students who set unrealistically high goals for improving their reading are disappointed when they fail to fulfill them.
3. The proximity of goals. The effectiveness of goals is largely determined by how far into the future they are projected. Proximal goals mobilize effort and direct what one does now. When the student focuses on the distant future, it is too easy to temporize efforts at change in the present. "One can always begin in earnest in the tomorrows of each day" (Bandura, 1985, pp. 10-11). Students with reading difficulties must establish short term goals they can accomplish realistically. These subgoals can be the basis for greater achievement in the future. They also provide con-

Gentile and McMillan

tinuous incentives and guides for self-regulation that build a sense of competence, self-satisfaction, and motivation. If students concentrate on improving their reading each day in class, in a year's time they will be well on the road to attaining their long term goals.

Self-Incentives. The second step in developing students' direct coping or self-regulating reading skills is to help them establish incentives to work and to provide themselves with tangible rewards when they reach established goals. Bandura (1985, p. 11) adds:

> People can get themselves to do things they would otherwise put off or avoid altogether by arranging incentives for subgoal attainments. They achieve greater self-directed change if they reward their successful efforts than if they provide no incentives for themselves. Evaluative self-incentives also serve as important self-motivators and guides for behavior. People get themselves to put forth the effort necessary to accomplish what they value for the satisfaction they derive from fulfilling goals they set for themselves.

Students' incentives are highly individual. It is important that teachers take the time to define each student's incentives. While some incentives can be used effectively for groups of students, the most powerful and sustaining are those identified by students themselves. Ultimately, there is a big difference between developing an inner desire to be an effective reader and being extrinsically motivated to read by rewards or punishments from teachers, parents, or peers.

Self-Monitoring. As a final step in helping students acquire coping or self-regulatory skills, teachers must help them monitor the behavior they seek to change (Kazdin, 1974). Encouraging students to keep track of their stress level and the events that foster it during reading serves several purposes. According to Bandura (1985, p. 9), "Observing covariations of behavior and the circumstances under which it occurs serves as a self-diagnostic device for identifying determinants of one's behavior. Self-monitoring also provides the information needed for setting realistic subgoals and for evaluating one's progress. Continuing feedback about how one is doing is essential in sustaining the process of change."

Sports provides a model for demonstrating the importance of self-monitoring. A weight lifter, for example, can record the increasing number of presses or curls and can see increased muscle structure. This positive feedback encourages continued effort and improvement (Horn, 1986). Teachers need to set up the same kind of circumstances for students during reading instruction.

Teachers or students can observe incremental gains in reading and provide feedback. To ensure long term effects, students with reading difficulties must have reasons to change and the means to do so. Neither goals without performance feedback nor performance feedback without goals achieves any lasting change (Bandura & Cervone, 1984).

Before positive changes can occur, students must recognize their problems, acknowledge the nature of those problems, and gain control using adaptive stress reducing behaviors. This means sizing up the situation accurately and attempting to solve problems.

Entwisle (1971) suggested that "control beliefs" are especially important in reading because middleclass parents teach their children to expect order and meaning in their daily lives and to develop alternative strategies for dealing with problems that appear to violate this order. Other children's early education may be deficient in these respects. When children expect reading to be a system with its own internal meaning and consistency as well as a tool to help solve other problems, they are often excited about learning to read. If children do not see reading as having these characteristics, it becomes "one more thing" imposed on unwilling victims by powerful authority figures.

The Teacher's Role

The teacher's role is crucial in creating an instructional environment that leads students to success, by modeling and by assisting students in developing attainable goals, providing consistent feedback, and eliciting self-evaluative information concerning reading performance. A structured, purposeful approach is vital to the process of self-regulation and remediation in reading.

Students with reading difficulties must learn to apply self-regulating skills steadily and consistently in attempting increasingly challenging and sometimes stressful assignments. Teachers must help students gain confidence in attempting more difficult reading tasks.

Immediate success is essential for students who have a history of difficulty or failure in reading. However, these students must gradually learn to struggle with adversity and to overcome their problems, even if they do encounter occasional failure.

Eventually students learn that their difficulty or failure in reading may be more attributable to a lack of effort than to a lack of ability or to external factors. Research on learned helplessness indicates that, with few exceptions, more reading difficulties result from students' lack of effort than from their lack of ability.

Teachers must work so these students

1. *Gain control over their reading responses.* Students need to identify their maladaptive stress reactions to reading and develop more successful strategies that help them approach and gain control. Only then can they experience success as readers.

2. *Gain confidence and competence as readers.* Students need to be shown how to apply the necessary skills to successfully complete reading assignments. This means more than mastering isolated skills; it means developing the necessary self-control and strategies to study and process written information for purposes of taking tests, making oral and written reports, and contributing to class discussions.

3. *Gain closure and learn to cope successfully with their reading difficulties through self-regulation.* This includes helping students overcome their fear or anger toward reading by identifying and reinforcing purposeful reading activities, mastering incremental learning steps, and establishing a schedule for accomplishing the work. Students cannot alter what has happened to them in the past, but they can pursue solutions to current problems through prediction, flexibility, concentration, careful preparation, and practice.

Typically, students with reading difficulties develop a perception of reading and of themselves as readers that is geared to failure. They expect to do poorly and to fail; consequently, they do both. Their apprehension makes them anxious enough to force these outcomes. Teachers are like good coaches. They must push students to do their best, sometimes beyond their abilities; help them overcome the fear of failure so they will take risks; and provide safety nets to catch them when they stumble. Teachers must also develop special relationships with these students, providing patience, understanding, and knowledge to help students achieve specific goals.

Summary

McGuiness (1986) said, "It is time that the research on learning to read and on acquiring self-control be brought into the mainstream and taught in teachers' colleges." Teachers working to help students overcome reading difficulties need to teach self-regulating skills as well as skills needed to decode and interpret print. Effective intervention can provide the basis for students to reach reading independence through self-correction and guidance. Students must be taught to set explicit, proximal, and reasonable goals; arrange rewards for their efforts; monitor their self-defeating fight or flight responses when reading is stressful for them; and use a variety of coping strategies instead of a single technique.

References

Allington, R.L. Poor readers don't get to read much in reading groups. *Language Arts,* 1980, *57* (8) 872-876.

Bandura, A. *Social learning theory.* Englewood Cliffs, NJ: Prentice-Hall, 1977.

Bandura, A. *Social learning theory.* Paper presented at the Carnegie Conference on Unhealthful Risk Taking Behavior in Adolescence, San Francisco, January 1985.

Bandura, A., and Cervone, D. *Differential engagement of self-reactive influences in motivation.* Unpublished manuscript, Stanford University, 1984.

Bird, G. Personality factors in learning. *The Personnel Journal,* 1927, *6,* 56-59.

Blanchard, P. Reading disabilities in relation to difficulties of personality and emotional development. *Mental Hygiene,* 1936, *20,* 384-413.

Cannon, W.B. *Bodily changes in pain, hunger, fear, and rage.* New York: Appleton-Century, 1915.

Deci, E.L. The well-tempered classroom—How not to motivate teachers and students: Impose stricter standards, more controls, and greater conformity. *Psychology Today,* March 1985, 52-53.

Dolch, E.W. *The psychology and teaching of reading.* Boston: Ginn, 1931.

Gentile and McMillan

Dolch, E.W. *The psychology and teaching of reading,* second edition. Champaign, IL: Garrard, 1951.

Dreikurs, R. Emotional predispositions to reading difficulties. *Archives of Pediatrics,* 1954, *71,* 340.

Dreikurs, R., and Soltz, V. *Children: The challenge.* New York: Hawthorn Books, 1964.

Entwisle, D.R. Implications of language socialization for reading models and for learning to read. *Reading Research Quarterly,* 1971, *7* (1), 111-167.

Freud, A. Psychoanalysis and the training of the young child. *Psychiatric Quarterly,* 1935, *4,* 15-24.

Gann, E. *Reading difficulty and personality organization.* New York: Kings Crown Press, 1945.

Gates, A.I. The role of personality maladjustment in reading disability. *Journal of Genetic Psychology,* 1941, *69,* 77-83.

Gentile, L.M., and McMillan, M.M. Profiling problem readers: Diagnosis and prescription. *Academic Therapy,* 1981, *17* (1), 47-56.

Gentile, L.M., and McMillan, M.M. *Stress and reading difficulties: Research, assessment, intervention.* Newark, DE: International Reading Association, 1987.

Gentile, L.M., and McMillan, M.M. *Stress as a factor in reading difficulties: From research to practice.* Paper presented at the American Reading Forum National Conference, Orlando, Florida, December 1984.

Gentile, L.M., McMillan, M.M., and Swain, C. Parents' identification of children's life crises: Stress as a factor in reading difficulties. In G. McNinch (Ed.), *Reading research in 1984: Comprehension, computers, communication.* Carrollton, GA: Thomasson Printing, 1985.

Hilgard, E.R., Atkinson, R.C., and Atkinson, R.L. *Introduction to psychology.* New York: Harcourt Brace Jovanovich, 1975, 442.

Horn, J.C. Pumping iron, pumping ego. *Psychology Today,* 1986, *20,* 16.

Johnston, P.H. Understanding reading disability. *Harvard Educational Review,* 1985, *55,* 153-177.

Kanfer, F.H. Self-management methods. In F.H. Kanfer and P. Goldstein (Eds.), *Helping people change: A textbook of methods.* New York: Pergamon, 1980, 334-389.

Kazdin, A.E. Self-monitoring and behavior change. In M.J. Mahoney and C.E. Thoresen (Eds.), *Self-control: Power to the person.* Monterey, CA: Brooks/Cole, 1974.

Lamb, P. *The symptoms of childhood depression as factors in children's reading difficulties.* Unpublished doctoral dissertation, North Texas State University, 1985.

Laurita, R.E. Child's reading ability linked to development of visual perception. *Education Week,* 1985, *5* (7), 18.

Locke, E.A., Shaw, K.N., Saari, L.M., and Latham, G.P. Goal setting and task performance: 1969-1980. *Psychological Bulletin,* 1981, *90,* 125-152.

Maxwell, M. The role of attitudes and emotions in changing reading and study skills behavior of college students. *Journal of Reading,* 1971, *14* (6), 359-364, 420-422.

McDermott, R.P. Social relations as contexts for learning. *Harvard Educational Review,* 1977, *47,* 198-213.

McGuiness, D. Facing the learning disabilities crisis. *Education Week,* 1986, *5,* 22-28.

Mehan, H. *Learning lessons.* Cambridge, MA: Harvard University Press, 1979.

Moffett, J. Hidden impediments to improving English teaching. *Phi Delta Kappan,* 1985, *67,* 50-56.

Natchez, G. *Personality patterns and oral reading: A study of overt behavior in the reading situation as it reveals reactions of dependence, aggression, and withdrawal in children.* New York: New York University Press, 1959.

Robinson, H.A. (Ed.). Meeting individual differences in reading. *Proceedings of the Annual Conference on Reading.* Chicago: University of Chicago Press, 1964.

Robinson, H.A. *Why pupils fail in reading.* Chicago: University of Chicago Press, 1946.

Runck, B. *Behavioral self-control: Issues in treatment assessment.* Rockville, MD: National Institute of Mental Health Science Reports, 1982.

Selye, H. *The stress of life.* New York: McGraw-Hill, 1956, 31-32.

Selye, H. *The stress of life,* revised edition. New York: McGraw-Hill, 1976.

Silverman, J.S., Fite, M.W., and Mosher, M.M. Clinical findings in reading disability children: Special cases of intellectual inhibition. *American Journal of Orthopsychiatry,* 1959, *29,* 298-314.

Spache, G.D. *Investigating the issues of reading disabilities.* Boston: Allyn and Bacon, 1976.

Swain, C. *Stress as a factor in primary schoolchildren's reading difficulties.* Unpublished doctoral dissertation, North Texas State University, 1985.

Weinberg, W., and Rehmet, A. Childhood affective disorder and school problems. In D.F. Cantwell and G.A. Carlson (Eds.), *Affective disorders in childhood and adolescence: An update.* Englewood Cliffs, NJ: Spectrum Publications, 1983.

White, R.W. Motivation reconsidered: The concept of competence. *Psychological Review,* 1959, *66,* 297-333.

Wiskell, W. The relationship between reading difficulties and psychological adjustment. *Journal of Educational Research,* 1948, *4* (7), 557-559.

Gentile and McMillan

A Dynamic-Developmental-Interaction Approach to Reading and Related Learning Disabilities

W hile most of this monograph is addressed to the issue of diagnostic procedures suitable in the assessment of reading *problems,* this chapter will focus on individuals who experience reading and related learning *disabilities.* To this end, I will define learning disabilities and show how they are differentiated from most learning problems. The term "learning disabilities" suggests the presence of some form of central nervous system dysfunction; reading disability is one type of learning disability. For individuals experiencing reading and related learning disabilities, a medical model in diagnostic assessment is most efficient. A multidisciplinary orientation is essential, along with a developmental approach in which the individual is evaluated and diagnosed in terms of the dynamic interaction of physical, cognitive, educational, social, and affective factors.

The graphic organizer gives some structure to this chapter.

The Problem of Definition

There is confusion concerning learning disability because of multiple and varying definitions. Historically, the term "learning disability" was first used by Kirk (1962), who stated that a learning disability refers to a retardation disorder, or delayed development in one or more of the processes of speech, language, hearing, spelling, writing, or arithmetic. Kirk indicated further that the disability resulted from possible cerebral dysfunction or emotional or behav-

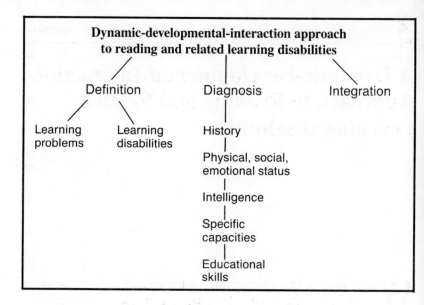

**Dynamic-developmental-interaction approach
to reading and related learning disabilities**

Definition
    Learning problems
    Learning disabilities

Diagnosis
    History
    Physical, social, emotional status
    Intelligence
    Specific capacities
    Educational skills

Integration

ioral disturbance. He excluded disabilities stemming from mental retardation, sensory deprivation, or cultural and instructional factors. Bateman (1965) described children with learning disabilities as those who manifest an educationally significant discrepancy between their estimated intellectual potential and actual level of performance. She related the disability to some basic disorder in the learning processes, which may be accompanied by demonstrable central nervous system dysfunction. She excluded those disabilities secondary to generalized mental retardation, educational or cultural deprivation, severe emotional disturbance, or sensory loss.

In 1968, the National Advisory Committee on Handicapped Children stated that learning disabilities may be manifested in disorders of listening, thinking, talking, reading, writing, spelling, or arithmetic. Learning disabilities include conditions referred to as perceptual handicaps, brain injury, minimal brain dysfunction, dyslexia, and developmental aphasia. They do not include learning problems due primarily to visual, hearing, or motor handicaps; to mental retardation or emotional disturbance; or to environmental disadvantage. This view of learning disabilities essentially constitutes the definition Congress used in Public Law 94-142: The Education for All Handicapped Children Act of 1975. This is the definition most widely used to identify pupils eligible for specific learning disability services. Numerous positive effects have been realized through the definition and general goals of PL 94-142. However, misinterpretations of the definition have resulted in a series of problems that have affected theoretical and service delivery issues in learning disabilities.

The National Joint Committee on Learning Disabilities (NJCLD) has commented (1981) on problems raised by the misinterpretations of the definition stated in PL 94-142. The NJCLD emphasizes that learning disability should be recognized as a general term referring to a heterogeneous group of disorders involving different subgroups of individuals. One must recognize the developmental nature of learning disabilities and view them as problems from early childhood into adult life. The NJCLD urges that disorders represented by the term "learning disabilities" be understood as intrinsic to the individual and that the basis of the disorders be presumed to be some form of central nervous system dysfunction. While the NJCLD supports the idea that failure to learn or to attain curricular expectations occurs for diverse reasons, learning disabilities have their basis in inherently altered processes of acquiring and using information. Finally, the NJCLD points out that the wording of the exclusion clause in the current definition of learning disabilities lends itself to the misinterpretation that individuals with learning disabilities cannot be multihandicapped or be from different cultural and linguistic backgrounds. Learning disabilities may occur concomitantly with other handicapping conditions.

In light of the points stated previously, the NJCLD (1981, p. 5) recommends the following definition of learning disabilities:

> Learning disabilities is a generic term that refers to a heterogeneous group of disorders manifested by significant difficulties in the acquisition and use of listening, speaking, reading, writing, reasoning or mathematical abilities. These disorders are intrinsic to the individual and presumed to be due to central nervous system dysfunction.

Even though a learning disability may occur concomitantly with other handicapping conditions (e.g., sensory impairment, mental retardation, social and emotional disturbance) or environmental influences (e.g., cultural differences, insufficient/inappropriate instruction, psychogenic factors), it is not the direct result of those conditions or influences.

The confusion regarding the definition of learning disability has resulted in wide variance in agreement of the incidence of the learning disabled. Figures on the incidence of learning disabilities within public schools range from 3 percent to 20 percent depending on the definition and types of factors used in deriving the figures. When learning disability is defined as in the statement of the NJCLD, the incidence is probably close to 3 percent. In counting children, Congress has stated that children with specific learning disabilities may not constitute more than one-sixth of the children counted as handicapped. Another limitation is that a state may not count as handicapped more than 12 percent of children aged five through seventeen. This means that for allocation purposes only 2 percent of the children in a state may be counted as having specific learning disabilities.

In summary, the following are some of the major points regarding the problem of definition:

1. The vast majority of children who are experiencing academic difficulty in school have learning problems, not learning disabilities. (See Gentile and McMillan, this volume.)

2. Most reading and related learning problems are caused by external factors; by largely environmental aspects. The most common causes are in the educational sphere: inappropriate teaching, nondifferentiated instruction, and overcrowded classrooms. Most of this monograph is intentionally addressed to the assessment procedures used in the diagnoses of reading/writing *problems.*

3. Some reading/learning problems may be the result of other environmental factors such as cultural deprivation or emotional blocking.

4. Learning disabilities are intrinsic to the individual and are presumed to be the result of some form of central nervous system dysfunction.
5. Learning disabilities are neither common nor rare. The incidence in the general school population is probably 2 percent to 5 percent.
6. Learning disabilities do not represent a homogeneous group of individuals. Rather, the term is a general one referring to a heterogeneous group of disorders realized as significant difficulties in the acquisition and use of one or more of the following functions: listening, speaking, reading, writing, reasoning, and mathematical abilities.
7. Reading disability is one type of learning disability. The incidence of reading disability in the general population is probably no more than 2 percent.
8. Reading and related learning disabilities can occur in early childhood, during the school years, and in adult life. The learning disability may be manifested in different ways at varying stages.
9. Sensory impairment and emotional difficulties may occur concomitantly with learning disabilities, but they are not the primary cause of the problem.
10. While all individuals should be provided appropriate educational services, one must neither deny the existence of nor overestimate the incidence of reading/learning disabilities.

Diagnostic Considerations

Among learning disability professionals, there is an increasing awareness of the need to move away from fragmentation and toward a more comprehensive and less divisive approach in the diagnosis of reading and related learning disabilities. This awareness stems partially from the realization that understanding deviant functions of learning disabled children comes from having a coherent theoretical framework that directs systematic investigations and integrates the data meaningfully (Senf, 1972). The efficacy of treatment and the prognosis depend on the validity of the diagnosis.

This, in turn, is contingent upon the accuracy of one's observations, the availability of a conceptual framework that permits the synthesis of those observations into a meaningful pattern, and the integration of that pattern into existing knowledge. Without objective observations and an appropriate conceptual framework, a valid diagnosis is not possible.

In using a dynamic-developmental-interaction approach to the diagnosis of learning disabilities, close attention must be given to the interaction, assimilation, accommodation, and integration of biological, psychological, social, economic, and educational factors. The individual is viewed as a physical organism functioning in a social environment in a psychological manner (Abrams, 1984).

It must be reemphasized that the population of learning disabled individuals addressed in this chapter are most frequently assessed in a one to one, clinical situation (such as a reading clinic, child guidance clinic, hospital). We assert that schools, in general, are responsible for recognizing and accommodating the wide variations of normal individual differences in learning. In the usual course of development there are also differences and delays that can interfere with the expected acquisition and use of academic skills. Students who show such variations should not immediately be thought of as having learning disabilities and referred for special help. In most cases, their needs should be addressed within regular education. One purpose of the assessment procedures is to make a differential diagnosis. That is, it is necessary to rule out conditions other than learning disabilities that may interfere with the individual's ability to function effectively in school. As stressed previously, a major objective of this type of diagnosis is to differentiate a learning problem from a learning disability.

The dynamic-developmental-interaction orientation in the diagnosis of learning disability requires a multidisciplinary approach. No one professional has the skills and knowledge necessary to evaluate, diagnose, recommend, or provide programs and services for the individual who is identified as having a learning disability. The major purposes of any diagnostic evaluation are to determine the existence and severity of the learning disability, the specific strengths and weaknesses, and the therapeutic steps needed to ameliorate the condition. For diagnosis to be effective, it must also result in accurate communication to the remedial clinician, the therapist, the school, and the parent of sufficient information about the problem so that a profitable program of habilitation or rehabilitation will result. If the only resultant in a thorough diagnostic procedure is an explanation of the difficulty, the process has been next to useless. For the child, the home, and the school, the problem is still one of finding a solution to the inadequate forms of adjustment that were the precipitating reasons for the referral in the first place.

In order to comprehend fully all of the factors contributing to the individual's reading or related learning disability, information must be obtained in five major areas. First, a detailed history is required to provide the contextual basis for understanding and interpreting all the clinical and test data obtained. Emphasis is on maturation and development with attention focused on the numerous biological and environmental factors that influence the child's physical, social, and cognitive growth. Second, there should be careful analysis of the individual's current physical, social, and emotional status. Third, an individually obtained assessment of the child's intelligence is required. One must keep in mind, however, that the intelligence quotient is not the sole measure of cognitive ability. Criteria based on IQ scores typically disregard intraindividual differences in performance with respect to different aspects of intellectual functioning. In addition, manifestations of learning disabilities can reduce performance on intelligence tests as well as on achievement measures. Fourth, there must be measures of specific capacity including perceptual motor skills, sensory functions, concept formation, problem solving, and memory span. Fifth, the picture with respect to achievement in each of the academic and communication areas involved must be detailed sufficiently to clarify the specific nature of students' difficulties and the resources available to them in meeting any learning demands.

History

Five highly related areas of significance bear careful objective study in obtaining a comprehensive history of the problem. The first of these pertains to the family constellation and the children's psychological role within the family group. Age, educational experience and achievement, occupation, general health, interests, hobbies, normal daily schedule, and general attitudes toward learning should be obtained for each person living in the home. A brief medical and social history of parents' families and the nature of the extended family support in the past and in the present also should be acquired.

Second, all facts pertinent to the prenatal, perinatal, and postnatal development must be obtained. Major importance is attributed to the record if, for example, the child was premature, or had neonatal bilirubin encephalopathy or meningitis in early infancy. One might also wish to have a detailed obstetrical history in making an initial assessment of possible brain lesions in the fullterm newborn. There is conflicting evidence concerning the effect of prolonged labor, precipitous delivery, and intracranial pressure at the time of birth caused by forceps delivery or a narrow pelvic arch in the mother.

Pasamanick and Knobloch (1961) have coined the term "reproductive casualty" to account for the sequelae of harmful events during pregnancy and the birth process. Most of the resulting damage to fetuses and newborn infants is in the central nervous system. Because fetal and neonatal deaths are largely associated with complications of pregnancy or prematurity, these potentially brain-damaging events might result in children who do not succumb, but go on to develop a series of neuropsychiatric disorders. Depending on the specific nature and extent of the insult to the brain, the disorders might range from gross neurologic impairment to the more subtle specific and nonspecific problems labeled minimal brain dysfunction or learning disability. It may be that the greater vulnerability of the male fetus and neonate may account for the higher incidence of learning problems among boys.

Intensive studies of neonates are being made, many dealing with those infants who fail to grow to normal size before birth. The survival of infants seems to be profoundly affected by the birth weight; the lower the weight of the newborn, the greater the danger he or she faces. Wessel (1979) presents data to support the construct of a continuum of reproductive casualty, in that certain types of delivery clearly increase the likelihood of later impaired or delayed performance. In addition, the findings of his investigation provide evidence that argues strongly for a dynamic-developmental-interaction approach to the diagnosis of learning disability. An analysis of Wessel's results supports the view that both constitutional and environmental factors are responsible for the impact of the birth process on the developmental status of the child. The use of at risk indicators should be only one step in determining the status and needs of the child. As the NJCLD (1985, p. 4) points out,

> At risk indicators do not always predict which child is in jeopardy of future developmental deficits or which aspects of development will be delayed or disordered. Caution should be used when informing parents about the presence of these indicators. For example, some children with a history of perinatal complications may develop normally, while other children without such histories may demonstrate specific patterns of deficits that will require careful assessment and intervention.

The maturational and developmental milestones should be explored carefully. Locomotion skills should be noted including the age of development of crawling, standing, and walking independently. Special attention should be paid to the development of speech and language, since the roots of most learning disabilities are found in the language area. For example, delay in oral language development is probably the best single indicator of probable difficulty in learning to read.

The third area of importance in the history pertains to the medical and psychological record. Accidents, illnesses, immunizations, hospitalizations, and behavioral characteristics noted preceding and following each of these instances should be included. It is often necessary for the clinician to follow up on a recorded medical episode or previous psychological evaluation by contacting the physician or psychologist involved in the treatment for additional data. Once again, episodes that appear to have bearings on subsequent neurological or communication functioning will be of particular significance.

Fourth, it is important to acquire as much information as possible about the social and emotional development of the child. Knowledge of the phases and stages of personality development is important in any assessment process of children with learning disabilities. Genetically, children's social and emotional adjustments are explored with questions related to their feeding habits, sleeping habits, nervous symptoms, early interpersonal relationships, and first experiences in school.

Finally, the entire school record is examined carefully. Children's social and emotional adjustments to fellow students and to their teacher are reviewed with as much care as their academic performance in each grade. Children's initial reactions to school; regularity of attendance; early symptoms of difficulty; attempts at that point to identify the problems and to provide assistance; referrals for diagnosis, tutoring, and remedial treatment—all may have bearing on their current difficulties and should be carefully recorded. Particular attention should be given to the age of onset of the problem.

Physical, Social, and Emotional Status

A thorough diagnosis of learning disability should include a visual screening designed to evaluate the coordinate functioning of the eyes. Specifically, the screening should be directed to detect problems of visual efficiency—that is, accommodation (clearness of vision), convergence (singleness of vision), and the relationship established between accommodation and convergence. The diagnosis and treatment of a visual problem belongs in the realm of the vision specialist who is trained to deal with such problems. But the diagnostician of reading and related learning disabilities should be equipped to screen out visual difficulty that may affect the child's ability to learn. Exclusive reliance on the Snellen Chart, which is only a measure of visual acuity, is inadequate for detecting problems that might contribute to learning difficulty. Such procedures as the Keystone Visual Screening Test, the Ortho-Rater, or the Massachusetts Vision Test offer more comprehensive methods to detect visual anomalies, since they especially assess all aspects of visual efficiency.

Hearing problems may play a role in the etiology of learning disabilities. Since, in most schools, reading is taught as a process whereby the child associates printed symbols with speech sounds, the student having a hearing loss may be readily confused. Some children do not experience any difficulty in auditory acuity, but are unable to discriminate between similar sounds (auditory discrimination). There is wide agreement that an individual audiometric examination should be used to screen for hearing defects. Further assessment of auditory acuity for children includes tests of speech-sound discrimination and informal observations.

It is difficult to interpret the minor signs that suggest some type of central nervous system dysfunction in a significant number of presumably normal children. Some representative signs are abnormal eye movements, clumsiness, visual-perceptual problems, and articulation defects. In recent years, neuropsychological evaluation has contributed greatly to our ability to diagnose learning disability and to determine if the problems are intrinsic to the individual or result form some environmental causation.

In assessing children's social and emotional status, the diagnostician is concerned with children's ability to see things as other people see them, their capacity to relate to other persons, and their effectiveness in dealing with their ideas and feelings in an adaptive manner. Clinicians attempt to learn how children cope with disturbing emotions. They explore the maneuvers children employ to bring about desired reactions from others; they also study the particular defense mechanisms children use that may facilitate or impede educational progress. Abrams (1968) states that the ego defense mechanisms are the most important emotional factors affecting learning. He feels that the emphasis in the assessment of the emotional status as it relates to learning disability should move away from the conflicts themselves to the ego defenses erected to cope with these conflicts.

Clinicians must also pay careful attention to the family constellation, how it may contribute to academic failure and be affected by or exacerbate a true learning disability. Abrams and Kaslow (1976, 1977) have written extensively about the role of family dynamics in sustaining learning disability. They pay particular attention to the hurt pride experienced by parents when their child does not measure up to their glamorized image of their child. The psychological preparation for a forthcoming child normally involves the fantasy of a perfect child, a kind of ego ideal. The parents may long for an offspring who possesses all of the characteristics they admire in themselves and who will not have all the traits they dislike in themselves. There is usually some disparity between the parents' dream child and the actual child. To accept and resolve this discrepancy becomes a developmental task of parenthood. It is an aspect in the evolution of a healthy mother-child relationship. But when the disparity is too great—as in the birth of a baby with a handicap, or where the parents' wishes are too unrealistic—this may be too much for the parents' coping mechanisms.

In addition to the clinical observations and the evaluation of the family constellation, psychological testing may make an important contribution to understanding the nature of the emotional factors concomitant with the learning disability. Frequently, this part of the assessment includes projective testing. In responding to relatively unstructured materials, individuals will project their own ideas and feelings, conflicts and anxieties, on these stimuli and thereby furnish an x ray of their personality. By carefully interpreting the results of projective tests as well as the objective measures, the clinician may gain important clues to children's general effectiveness in a learning situation.

Assessment of Intelligence

It is axiomatic that a comprehensive clinical diagnosis requires the administration of an individual intelligence test. Although a number of such instruments are available, those devised by David Wechsler are most commonly used. In cases of reading disability, they are particularly appropriate, since they combine measures of verbal and nonverbal intellectual abilities and provide a scattering of subtests measuring specific abilities that appear to be highly related to difficulties in reading. In addition to the overall intelligence score and the comparison between verbal and performance tests as a whole, those subtests related to concept formation, vocabulary development, perceptual abilities, memory span, and visual-motor associational skills are often particularly helpful to the clinician.

Although pattern analysis is frequently used in diagnosing learning disabilities, one must exercise considerable caution. There are clusters of test patterns associated with different types of reading disabilities, but this kind of analysis is effective only when it is carried out in a perceptive, nonbiased manner with attention given to the quality of the verbalizations and the behavioral observations as well. With this caution in mind, one can more profitably use an intelligence test to detect certain perceptual and conceptual deficiencies that are frequently manifested in learning disability syndromes. Denker (1964) has discussed the kinds of errors made by the typically braindamaged child; Abrams (1975), the intellectual patterning expected in two types of dyslexics; and Pikulski (1978), the implications of intelligence-test findings in a variety of cases of reading disability.

As stated previously, neuropsychologists have made a significant contribution to our understanding of the unique characteristics of the learning disabled individual. The neuropsychological model includes traditional psychosocial knowledge and skills, but also uses an additional body of complex knowledge and clinical skills to provide a better understanding of behavior and learning problems that include neurogenic variables. The neuropsychological contribution has been particularly valuable in differentiating subtypes of reading disability. Specifically, with regard to intellectual assessment, two different types of developmental dyslexia have been identified. In the auditory linguistic dyslexic, there is a significantly lower verbal IQ than performance IQ. This group also shows the so-called ACID pattern (Rourke, 1981). This is characterized by outstandingly poor performance on the WISC Arithmetic, Coding, Information, and Digit Span subtests. This pattern tends to have a very poor prognosis with respect to eventual recovery from reading retardation (Ackerman, Dykman, & Peters, 1976). In the visual-spatial dyslexic, the performance IQ is significantly lower than the verbal IQ. The learning disabled individual typically has difficulty on the Block Design, Object Assembly, and Picture Completion subtests.

A good clinician uses the results of an intelligence test in much the same way as a detective uses clues to solve a mystery.

Nothing is left to chance or just considered an anomaly. Every subtest score, every response, and every part of every response must be viewed as significant and as representative of the subject. For example, there are individuals with learning disabilities who appear to manifest problems not in decoding (as we find in dyslexics), but in integration (conceptual difficulties). It is not at all unusual for a child to respond to a question such as "What are the four seasons of the year?" with "Winter, Summer, June, and July."

Assessment of Specific Capacities

Perceptual motor abilities, while measured to some extent in certain subtests of the Wechsler scales, bear further evaluation. The Bender Visual-Motor Gestalt Test (1938) is the most frequently used measure of perceptual motor functioning. Several variations of the original procedure for administrating and scoring this instrument have been developed. The results are often used (sometimes incorrectly) to recommend a program of perceptual training. In fact, poor performance on the Bender Gestalt test may be ascribed to a number of different factors: perceptual deficit alone, motor dysfunction, inefficient coordination of visual and motor processes, anxiety interference, or simply negativism on the part of the child.

The Frostig Developmental Test of Visual Perception (1963) assesses five areas that may be related to academic skills: figure-ground relationships, eye-hand coordination, form constancy, position in space, and spatial relationships. Motor skills are necessary for adequate performance in each subtest. The DTVP yields a "perceptual quotient" with norms for children from ages four to seven. However, there is little evidence to suggest that the Frostig actually has the diagnostic ability to measure five separate visual perception skills. Some have also questioned whether the skills measured by the Frostig are significantly related to achievement in school.

In describing individuals with learning disability of the integrative type, Rappaport (1961) describes both perceptual and conceptual difficulties. There is some impairment in the areas of spatial relationships and spatial organization, figure-ground relationships, sequencing skills, visual imagery, visual-motor functioning, memory, skip counting, and an inability to correct an error in a perform-

Abrams

ance even after recognizing it. Under conceptual difficulties one might encounter associative word finding problems related to poor word retrieval, inadequate auditory processing skills, and difficulty in organizing a verbal response. Some children may make an arbitrary guess to the question rather than admit not knowing the answer.

Difficulties with attention and concentration may be related to learning disabilities. Although some memory abilities are involved in responding to most individual test items in any area, a specific memory span battery is helpful in identifying the nature of the individual's ability to attend to and retain stimuli experienced in different modalities. The Wechsler Memory Scale (1942) or specific subtests selected from the Detroit Tests of Learning Aptitude-2 (Hammill, 1985) are often employed. Tests used to measure attention and concentration should be composed of both discrete and related items as well as stimuli presented in various modalities (visual, auditory, or a combination of these).

Using primarily neuropsychological evaluation, Pirozzolo (1981) identified specific characteristics of the homogeneous subtypes of dyslexia within a heterogeneous population. The children falling into the auditory-linguistic subtype show developmentally delayed language onset; articulation disorders; anomia, object naming or color naming defects; reading errors involving the phonological aspects of language; spelling errors characteristic of poor phoneme to grapheme correspondence; and letter by letter decoding strategy. The children falling into the visual-spatial subtype of dyslexia show right-left disorientation; finger agnosia; spatial dysgraphia (poor handwriting, poor use of space); reading errors involving visual aspects; spelling errors characterized by letter and word reversals; the use of a phonetic decoding strategy; and faulty eye movements during reading.

Assessment of Educational Skills

The educational evaluation of the child is of utmost importance in determining the nature of the habilitative and remedial steps to be pursued. It is the responsibility of the clinician to discern where the child is functioning in all aspects of language development, such as listening, speaking, reading, and writing. More specifically, one must appraise (1) how well the child's current achievement compares with intelligence level; (2) how performance matches the performance of other children of the same age; (3) what level of material the child can be expected to read independently and where the most profit from instruction will result (not to mention where there will be frustrations determined by the complexity of the material); and (4) how well evaluation of personal performance and awareness of personal deficiencies is made.

Answers to many of the questions stated above can frequently be elicited by the intelligent use of formal inventories. Although the group reading inventory provides a valuable instrument for determining levels of performance, a much more thorough and diagnostic method is to appraise the performance of each pupil individually. In essence this procedure consists of having the child read orally at sight and then silently from a series of reading selections that increase in order of difficulty. Comprehension is checked by means of factual, inferential, and vocabulary questions. Information regarding achievement levels and specific deficiencies in language and reading can be gleaned from the proper administration of an informal reading inventory.

Individuals with severe reading disabilities most frequently experience difficulty in decoding. Dyslexia is not characterized by satisfactory decoding and poor comprehension. Word substitution, reversal of letter sequence, and letter or word omission, as well as slow rate, are commonly observed. Often the child has tremendous difficulty in acquiring an adequate sight vocabulary for reading. Boder (1973) has suggested that analysis of the types of errors in reading and spelling may provide a classification of dyslexics as having visual or auditory processing difficulties, or both. The dysphonetic dyslexia group reflects a primary deficit in letter-sound integration and in the ability to develop phonetic skills. Lacking phonetic skills, these children are unable to decipher words not in their sight vocabulary. The dyseidectic dyslexia group reflects a primary deficit in the ability to perceive whole words as gestalts. These children read phonetically, sounding out most words as if they were being encountered for the first time. The alexia group reflects a primary deficit in both the ability to develop phonetic word analysis (synthesis skills) as well as in the ability to perceive letters and whole words as visual gestalts. This child can be differentiated from the dysphonetic child by a significantly lower sight vocabulary, and from the dyseidetic child by a lack of word analysis skills. It is clear that Boder's classification is similar in many ways to Pirrazola's subtypes although the data are derived from a different kind of evaluation.

Summary

In the dynamic-developmental-interaction approach to the diagnosis of reading and related learning disabilities, we have stressed the importance of a multidisciplinary orientation. Competent assessment procedures require that the child be evaluated with a sound conceptual framework. There are many possible pitfalls in the evaluation of any individual with a learning disability. It is certainly important that the observations and testing be perceptive and accurate. The interpretation of both clinical and test findings depends to a large extent upon the competence of the diagnostician.

To summarize, there are significant requisites for applying the dynamic-developmental-interaction approach to the diagnosis of reading disability:

1. The individual with disability must be viewed in a holistic fashion with attention paid to the biological, psychological, and social processes in complex interaction with one another.
2. There should be a recognition of the differentiation between reading problems and reading disability.
3. It must be recognized that reading disability is one of many types of learning disability; learning disabilities are heterogeneous in nature.
4. There are different subtypes of reading disability which require different types of remediation and intervention.
5. Sensitivity and skill are essential in obtaining a longitudinal history from reliable informants.
6. The case history provides the contextual framework in which to understand our clinical observations and test results.

7. The evaluation procedures must attend to the emotional concomitants of the disability as well as the cognitive factors.

8. The multidisciplinary perspective allows the diagnostician(s) to give equal consideration to all the factors which affect and sustain reading disability.

9. It is the manner in which the contact with the child is maintained that determines the success or failure more than anything else.

10. A psychodynamic, affective approach to individuals with reading disability must replace the more traditional orientation, which has separated the cognitive from the emotional realm, a dichotomy that is superficial.

References

Abrams, J.C. Interaction of neurological and emotional factors in learning disability. *Learning Disabilities*, 1984, *3*, 27-37.

Abrams, J.C. Minimal brain dysfunction and dyslexia. *Reading World*, 1975, *14*, 219-227.

Abrams, J.C. The role of personality defenses in reading. In G. Natchez (Ed.), *Children with reading problems*. New York: Basic Books, 1968, 77-79.

Abrams, J.C., and Kaslow, F. Family systems and the learning disabled child: Intervention and treatment. *Journal of Learning Disabilities*, 1977, *10*, 27-31.

Abrams, J.C., and Kaslow, F. Learning disability and family dynamics: A mutual interaction. *Journal of Clinical Child Psychology*, 1976, *5*, 35-40.

Ackerman, P.T., Dykman, R.A., and Peters, J.E. Hierarchical factor patterns on the WISC as related to areas of learning deficits. *Perceptual and Motor Skills*, 1976, *42*, 583-615.

Bateman, B. An educator's view of a diagnostic approach to learning disorders. In J. Hellmuth (Ed.), *Learning disorders*, volume 1. Seattle, WA: Special Child Publications, 1965, 44-62.

Bender visual motor gestalt test. New York: Psychological Corporation, 1938.

Boder, E. Developmental dyslexia: A diagnostic approach based on three atypical reading spelling patterns. *Developmental Medicine and Child Neurology*, 1973, *15*, 663-687.

Decker, R.J. Manifestations of the brain damage syndrome in historical and psychological data. In S.R. Rappaport (Ed.), *Childhood aphasia and brain damage: A definition*. Narberth, PA: Livingston, 1964, 52-57.

Frostig, M. *Frostig developmental test of visual perception*. Consulting Psychologists Press, 1963.

Hammill, D.D. *Detroit tests of learning aptitude-2*. Austin, TX: Pro-Ed, 1985.

Kirk, S.A. *Educating exceptional children*. Boston: Houghton Mifflin, 1962.

National Advisory Committee on Handicapped Children. *Special education for handicapped children*, first annual report. Washington, DC: U.S. Department of Health, Education and Welfare, 1968.

National Joint Committee on Learning Disabilities. *Learning disabilities: Issues on definition*. Baltimore, MD: Orton Dyslexic Society, 1981.

National Joint Committee on Learning Disabilities. *Learning disabilities and the preschool child*. Baltimore, MD: Orton Dyslexic Society, 1985.

Abrams

Pasamanick, G., and Knobloch, H. Epidemiologic studies on the complications of pregnancy and the birth process. In G. Caplan (Ed.), *Prevention of mental disorders in childhood.* New York: Basic Books, 1961.

Pikulski, J. Factors related to reading problems. In R. Stauffer, J.C. Abrams, and J. Pikulski (Eds.), *Diagnosis, correction, and prevention of reading disabilities.* New York: Harper & Row, 1978, 163-195.

Pirozzolo, F.J. Language and brain: Neuropsychological aspects of developmental reading disability. *School Psychology Review,* 1981, *10,* 350-355.

Rappaport, S.R. Behavior disorder and ego development in a brain-injured child. *Psychoanalytic Study of the Child,* 1961, *16,* 423-450.

Rourke, B.P. Neuropsychological assessment of children with learning disabilities. In S.B. Filskov and T.J. Boll (Eds.), *Handbook of clinical neuropsychology.* New York: John Wiley & Sons, 1981, 453-498.

Senf, G.M. An information integration theory and its application to normal reading acquisition and reading disability. In N.D. Bryand and C.E. Kass (Eds.), *Leadership training institute in learning disabilities: Final report.* Tucson, AZ: University of Arizona, 1972, 51-56.

Wechsler memory scale. New York: Psychological Corporation, 1942.

Wessel, K. *A prospective study of the relationship between the type of delivery and the use of medication and learning disabilities and ego disturbances in children.* Unpublished doctoral dissertation, Johns Hopkins University, 1979.

4

Holistic Assessment of Coding Ability

This chapter describes informal holistic methods by which teachers can observe students' developing mastery of the coding system as they learn to read and write. The suggested methods depart from traditional ones that use nonsense syllables or words in isolation to assess coding ability separate from the other language processes that all readers and writers must use if they are to make sense of print. The chapter has two major thrusts: looking carefully at children's early writing and listening carefully to their oral reading.

According to K. Goodman (1986, p. 38), "Three language systems interact in written language: the graphophonic (sound and letter patterns), the syntactic (sentence patterns), and the semantic (meanings)." Of the three, only the graphophonic (coding) system is unique to written language. For those who espouse a holistic point of view, however, examining the graphophonic system is not possible without attention to the other systems and to the pragmatic context in which they are being used. Even a separate chapter focusing on coding is somewhat suspect, perhaps because of simplistic claims by Rudolf Flesch and others that mastery of the coding system *is* all there is to learning to read. Beliefs like these have resulted in early reading materials that present the coding system to children in meaningless fragments, divorced from context and meaning.

I believe it is important for children to master the coding system and to use it automatically. I believe with Perfetti (1984, p. 56, that "acquisition of the alphabetic code is a critical component — indeed the definitive component — of reading in an alphabetic language." Knowledge of how the coding system works can have

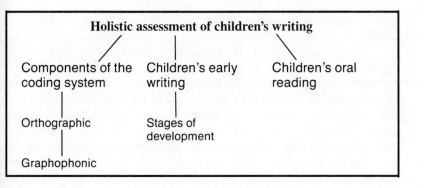

Holistic assessment of children's writing

- Components of the coding system
  - Orthographic
  - Graphophonic
- Children's early writing
  - Stages of development
- Children's oral reading

tremendous advantages for every learner—not just those at risk—and, according to Perfetti, there are "no known negative consequences" to helping children understand the system. Resnick (1979, p. 329) agrees, noting that "as a matter of routine practice, we need to include systematic, code oriented instruction in the primary grades, no matter what else is also done. This is the only place in which we have any clear evidence for any particular practice." She goes on to state that we cannot afford to ignore that evidence, but we also cannot assume that merely mastering the code will solve all reading problems. She suggests that a code *and* language emphasis are needed for successful literacy programs.

Whole language proponents do not dismiss the evidence presented, but they believe instructional programs can be organized so that mastery of the coding system can occur naturally. (See K. Goodman, 1986 and Holdaway, 1979 for suggestions on how this might be done.) Goodman (1986, p. 38) believes children will discover the alphabetic principle when they learn to write. "Whole language programs and whole language teachers do not ignore phonics; rather, they keep it in the perspective of real reading and real writing." Whole language programs have not been tried in this country, and there are few studies that offer evidence of their effectiveness. Because these programs emphasize the interactive nature of learning and build on the strengths that children bring with them, they hold great promise. In one study, children at risk were immersed in a language and print rich environment characterized by many opportunities to observe, try out, and practice literacy skills. They performed significantly better on both informal and standardized tests than those who were offered a typically fragmented and less meaningful worksheet approach (Taylor, Blum, & Logsdon, 1986).

Documentation of effectiveness of whole language programs for all children is still to come. Some poor readers who have been through the programs now available (and which are used by 90-95 percent of teachers) have not mastered the coding system. Olson and his colleagues (1984) report their study of disabled readers that showed them to be deficient in phonological coding. Liberman and Shankweiler (1985) report studies indicating that illiterate adults have difficulty with the coding system, indicating that insight does not necessarily accompany age and exposure. Breaking the code — mastering the graphophonic system, understanding the alphabetic principle, and recognizing familiar orthographic patterns — is important. Children who do not acquire these insights are at risk for learning to read.

What do beginning readers of any age need to know in order to master the coding system, and how can we tell whether these things are being learned?

Components of the Coding System

According to Y. Goodman (1984), one of the major roots of literacy is conscious awareness of its function, form, and context as evidenced in certain basic principles. Understanding the coding system begins with exploring the *relational* principles, or as Y. Goodman (p. 105) puts it, "understanding that some unit of written language represents some unit of meaning." Ferreiro and Teberosky (1982) documented the development of this understanding and concluded that children appear to progress in seven levels of interpretation, as follows:

Level 1. Children do not differentiate between a drawing and written language.
Level 2. Children begin to make this differentiation.
(However, Gibson and Levin, 1975, report studies indicating that few three year olds are unable to do this, even when the writing is in an unfamiliar language and when they come from an environment that is not print rich, e.g., the Yucatan.)

Level 3. Children begin to use the symbols prevalent in their culture's orthography. They may write only strings of numbers and letters, but "read" from these as text, telling their own stories.

Level 4. Children create their own interpretation of how the spoken language is related to written language. (Y. Goodman, 1984, provides an example with the story of Eric, age four, who read "cee-ree-ull," stretching out the syllable until he had finished pointing to the words Kellogg's Raisin Bran.)

Level 5. Children begin to use a syllabic hypothesis, one symbol to represent one syllable.

Level 6. Children combine both a syllabic and an alphabetic hypothesis. (This level has been analyzed extensively by several researchers—Gentry, 1982; Henderson & Beers, 1980; Read, 1975—who have studied how early writers use the coding system.)

Level 7. Children break the code and begin the discovery of the conventional spellings used in their respective orthographies.

Understanding the coding system begins with understanding the functional principle of literacy. Most children will read environmental print in ways that indicate their awareness of the functions of print long before they go to school. They may indicate that a stop sign says "don't go," for example, or that a Shell sign says "gas," or that a Colgate label says "toothpaste." As Heath (1982) has demonstrated, parents' attitudes toward print and the ways they use it help develop functional principles in their children.

Central to mastering the coding system is children's understanding of the linguistic principles of literacy. According to Y. Goodman (1984, p. 108), "Evidence shows that children hypothesize about all the linguistic cueing systems needed for written language. The orthographic system—including directionality, spelling, punctuation, and form variations, as well as the graphophonic system—*is new to children*. The phonologic, syntactic, semantic, and pragmatic systems are developed through oral language use, and children exhibit a growing awareness of how these systems operate differently under the constraints of written language."

In order to master the coding system, then, children must actually understand the orthographic and the graphophonic component systems.

The Orthographic System

Mastery of the orthographic system implies an understanding of basic concepts about print — important learnings that are often taken for granted by teachers but can seriously impede progress if children are confused about them (Clay, 1979; Holdaway, 1979). Indications of mastery of the orthographic system are the recognition of common English spelling patterns or chunks, the knowledge that only certain letter strings are allowable in English (words commonly end, but never begin with *ng*), and the immediate recognition of high frequency words as wholes.

To assess children's developing awareness of many aspects of the orthographic system, Clay (1979) offers her Sand and Stones tests, small booklets designed to measure basic concepts about print. An objection to these tests is the use of mutilated text. The following suggestions, adapted from Holdaway (1979), aid teachers with informal assessment.

1. Hand the child a book (spine pointing to the child) and ask the child to open it. Does the child know the spine goes on the left?
2. Ask the child to show you where you should begin reading. Does the child know the story begins where the print begins?
3. Ask where you should go next. Does the child know that the left hand page comes before the right hand page? That you move from the top to the bottom of the page? That you begin at the left and go along the line to the right and that you return to the next line on the left margin?
4. Give the child two index cards and ask him or her to frame one word; two words; one letter; two letters. Does the child know the concepts of word and letter?

5. Show the child a period, a question mark, a comma, an exclamation mark, quotation marks, and an apostrophe and ask what they are for. Does the child know?
6. Can the child follow a line of print in an enlarged text using word spaces?
7. Does the child use the concept of word fit? That is, does she or he know when there are too many or too few words?
8. Does the child realize that texts remain the same; that print is a stable word by word record of language?
9. Does the child understand the consistency principle, that the same word always has the same spelling?

Using these questions to guide reflective observation should help determine children's developing mastery of the orthographic system.

The Written Language Awareness Test cited by Taylor, Blum, and Logsdon (1986) also appears to be a useful tool for examining some aspects of orthographic awareness. It measures "the ability to segment oral sentences into their component words, the understanding that the spoken word is a cue to the length of the printed word, awareness of the technical aspects of written language and familiarity with the orientation of books, and attention to and use of graphic information in a cloze situation" (p. 134). As with all tests, the pragmatics of the situation and the meaningfulness of the tasks must be considered.

The Graphophonic System

Mastery of the graphophonic system entails an understanding of the relationship between speech and print. As Ehri (1979, p. 63) has written "If the light were not so gradual in dawning, the relationship between speech and print might count as one of the most remarkable discoveries of childhood." In educational terms (which often ignore basic prerequisite understandings), understanding the graphophonic system has been taken to mean understanding the idea that letters have some relationship to speech sounds, commonly called phonics. However, Wallach and Wallach (1979) and Haddock

(1976, 1978) have documented the importance of being sure children go beyond associating a particular sound with a particular letter to understanding the idea of segmentation and recombining as part of their learning of the alphabetic principle. Children need to understand the basic idea that sounds and letters are reusable. When the *m* is segmented from *mother,* for example, you can substitute *br* and get a whole new word—*brother.* Children who understand this segmenting and recombining principle are well on their way to understanding how the graphophonic system works; those who do not are likely to have great difficulty learning to read (see Lundberg, 1985; Olson et al., 1984; Wallach & Wallach, 1979).

In addition to obtaining clues about children's basic understandings about print, observing their early writing and listening to their reading provide insights about their understanding of the graphophonic system.

Children's Early Writing

K. Goodman (1986) suggests that children will acquire the coding system as they begin to write. It has been recommended that the writing process become a part of all literacy programs beginning with kindergarten (see Calkins, 1986; Graves, 1982 for specific procedures on how to undertake such programs). If writing precedes reading as Chomsky (1979) has implied, teachers should be able to examine children's writing for indications of their understanding of the orthographic and graphophonic systems and make hypotheses about their understanding of code in their reading as well. An examination of children's writing reveals many of their basic understandings of concepts about print, knowing that it is print that "tells the story" or the intricate aspects of directionality. Children's writing also reveals their understanding of concepts of letters (they generally begin with uppercase), spaces (they generally begin with none), words, letters, and punctuation marks. Bissix (1980) provides two wonderful examples of her son Paul's developing mastery of the orthographic system: RUDF (Are you deaf?!) at five years, one month, and EFUKANOPNKAZIWILGEVUAKNOPENR (If you can open cans I will give you a can opener) at five years, 2 months.

It is possible that teachers can learn much about their students' developing mastery of the graphophonic system (including their memory for sound-letter correspondences and their ability to segment and recombine) by examining their invented spellings and listening for comments about their discoveries about print as they learn to write. Flores and Garcia (1984) developed a checklist based on the developmental stages suggested by Ferriero and Teberosky (listed earlier in this chapter), but I believe an intensive analysis of Level 6 (children combine both a syllabic and an alphabetic hypothesis to represent units of meaning) will yield additional useful information regarding children's use of the coding system. Analyses of children's invented spellings by several researchers (Beers & Henderson, 1977; Gentry, 1982; Henderson & Beers, 1980; Read, 1975) have revealed developmental stages in children's early spelling and writing that reflect their hypotheses about how the coding system works. If teachers use the following stages (adapted from Gentry, 1982) as part of their checklists (see Figure), they should acquire insights into children's developing mastery of both the orthographic (OG) and graphophonic (GP) aspects of the coding system. Gentry's descriptions of the stages are interspersed with the comments of Morris (1984) who used similar stages to document the development of children's concepts of words.

Stage 1. Precommunicative Stage

At the Precommunicative Stage, the beginning writer
1. Demonstrates some knowledge of the alphabet by using letter forms to represent a message. (OG)
2. Shows no evidence of knowledge of letter-sound correspondences. The writing appears to be a random stringing together of letters that may also include number symbols. (OG)
3. May or may not use the principle of left-to-right directionality. (OG)
4. May know only a few letters which s/he repeats over and over or may evidence substantial knowledge of the alphabet. (OG)
5. May mix upper and lowercase letters indiscriminately, but tends to show a preference for uppercase. (OG)

Checklist for Developmental Stages in Early Writing*

Name _____ Age _____ Grade _____

	I	II	III	IV

Precommunicative Stage   *Date*

1. Produces letters or letter like forms to represent a message.
2. Includes number symbols as part of message.
3. Demonstrates left-to-right concept.
4. Demonstrates top-bottom concept.
5. Repeats known letters and numbers.
6. Uses many letters and/or numbers.
7. Mixes upper and lowercase letters.
8. Indicates preference for uppercase forms.

The Semiphonetic Stage   Date

1. Realizes letters represent sounds.
2. Represents whole words with one or more letters.
3. Evidence of letter name strategy.
4. Demonstrates left-to-right sequence of letters.
5. Puts spaces between words.

The Phonetic Stage   Date

1. Represents every sound heard.
2. Assigns letters based on sounds as child hears them. (invented spellings)
3. Puts spaces between words.
4. Masters letter formation.

The Transitional Stage   Date

1. Utilizes conventional spellings.
2. Vowels appear in every syllable.
3. Evidence of visual as opposed to phonetic strategy.
4. Reverses some letters in words.

Comments _____

_____

_____

_____

*Adapted from J. Richard Gentry, An analysis of developmental spelling in GNYS AT WRK. *The Reading Teacher*, 1982, *36*, 192-199.

Stage 2. Semiphonetic Stage

In the Semiphonetic Stage, the beginning writer

1. Begins to conceptualize that letters have sounds that are used to represent the sounds of words. (GP)
2. Uses letters to represent words which provide a partial mapping of phonetic representation for the word spelled. Semiphonetic spelling is abbreviated; one, two, or three letters may represent the whole word, e.g., MZR (monster). (GP)
3. Evidences a letter name strategy. Where possible, the writer represents words, sounds, or syllables with letters that match their letter names, e.g., R (are); U (you); LEFT (elephant), instead of representing the vowel and consonant sounds separately. This is Ferreiro and Teberosky's Level 5 (children begin to use a syllabic hypothesis — one symbol to represent one syllable). (GP)
4. Begins to grasp the left-to-right sequential arrangement of letters in English orthography. (OG)
5. Evidences greater knowledge of the alphabet and greater mastery of letter formation. (OG)
6. May or may not begin to leave spaces between words. (OG)

Within the semiphonetic stage (or prephonetic as he calls it), Morris (1984) suggests there are three substages. Prephonetic spellers usually begin with the beginning letter of a word, then add the ending letter, but can't give the vowel. They often omit it or (exhibiting orthographic awareness, there's something in the middle) put in a filler vowel. A prephonetic speller might spell *back* as *b, bc,* or *boc.*

Stage 3. Phonetic Stage

At the Phonetic Stage, the beginner writer

1. Is able to provide a total mapping of letter-sound correspondences; all of the surface sound features of the words are represented in the writing. (GP)
2. Systematically develops particular spellings for certain details of phonetic form. In representing short vowels, phonetic spellers often categorize the short vowel they are trying to spell with the nearest long vowel in place of artic-

ulation; then they use the long vowel letter name in the spelling. For example, both the short *i* and the long *e* sounds are produced in the high front part of the vocal tract. Therefore, when children attempt to represent the short *i* sound in *stick,* they substitute the letter name of the nearest vowel, *e,* producing the spelling *sek.* Likewise, a phonetic speller attempting to spell *bed* will often produce *bad,* categorizing short *e* and long *a* together (both mid-front vowels) and using the letter name *A* in the spelling. Phonetic stage spellers also omit vowels when they are not heard in a syllable (e.g., *table − tabl*) and nasals (*m* and *n*) when they precede stop consonants (e.g. *stamp − stap* or *sink − sek*). According to Morris, a phonetic speller would spell *back* as *bac* or *bak.* Children at this stage indicate extreme sensitivity to phonetic principles like affrication. For example, the point of articulation for the *t* in *trick* is the same as in *ch,* and both are affricates. Some children pick up on these similarities and spell *ash tray* as *as chray* and *tarantula* as *chrachela.* This same sensitivity is exhibited in their spelling of intervocalic flaps, which occur when an alveolar stop (*d* or *t*) intervenes between two vowels if the preceding vowel carries a greater degree of stress than the following one. In this position, there is no contrast between the *t* and the *d* − both are realized as a short tap of the tongue on the alveolar ridge. Because this flap is almost always voiced, it is phonetically closer to *d.* Examples cited by Read (1975) include *prede* for pretty, *bodom* for bottom, *adsavin* for eighty-seven, and *gadichans* for get a chance. Examples from a child's recounting of a trip to the zoo include *cheda* and *ciyode.* (GP)

3. Assign letters strictly on the basis of sounds, without regard for acceptable English letter sequence or other conventions of English orthography. More zoo examples included *glopcis todl* (Galapagos turtle), *pcoc* (peacock, *spidr monces* and *ranatags.* (GP)

4. Generally (but not always) use conventional spacing between words. (GP)

Paying particular attention to what children say as they write can reveal their developing awareness of the alphabetic principle of segmenting and recombining, a learning Ehri (1987, p. 15) believes contributed to the transfer of instruction in spelling certain words to children's ability to read those words. Bissex (1980) gives an excellent example of this. She noticed that as her son Paul was writing he said "You spell 'book' B-O-O-K. To write 'look' you just change one letter; take away the *B* and add an *L*." According to Gentry, these mental spellings and rehearsals (Paul also observed that "if you take the *T* and *R* off 'trike' and put a *B* in front, you have "bike' ") prepared him for the next stage of spelling.

Stage 4. Transitional Stage

At the transitional stage, the beginning writer

1. Adheres to basic conventions of English orthography: Vowels appear in every syllable; nasals are represented before consonants; both vowels and consonants are employed instead of a letter-name strategy; a vowel is represented before syllabic *r* even though it is not heard or felt as a separate sound; common English letter sequences are used in spelling, especially liberal use of vowel digraphs like *ai, ea, ay, ee,* and *ow;* silent *e* pattern becomes fixed as an alternative for spelling long vowel sounds; inflectional endings like *s, 's, ing,* and *est* are spelled conventionally. An interesting example of anticipating this stage was the writer who visited the zoo. He spelled *cage* as *caga,* either exhibiting orthographic awareness that something came after the *g* or representing something he heard as he attempted the spelling as in *cage-uh.* In the transitional stage this *e* is represented correctly.

2. Presents evidence of a new visual strategy – the child moves from phonological to morphological and visual spelling. (OG)

3. May include all appropriate letters, although some may be reversed. Many teachers will recognize this stage as the one when they get notes saying "I love yuo, Ms. Mr. _____ ." (OG)

Morris notes that transitional spellers move to a more abstract, if still nonstandard, representation of English words. These transitional spellings, which begin to appear in late first or early second grade, are to be welcomed by the teacher because they signal emergence of an underlying abstract word knowledge. Transitional spellers would probably spell *back* correctly, according to Morris, but examples of other transitional spellings might be *fete* for *feet* or *tabel* for *table*.

It appears that by using the stages explicated by Gentry (1982) and Morris (1984) and by examining even the earliest writing attempted by children, teachers can determine what kinds of hypotheses their students are making about all aspects of both the orthographic and graphophonic components of the coding system. To check awareness of the orthographic system, they can, through careful observation, gather evidence indicating their students are distinguishing print from drawing, beginning to understand the intricacies of directionality, developing a growing awareness of the function of spaces and word boundaries, beginning to control letter forms, developing understanding of the uses of punctuation, and using invariant spellings for common words and patterns. To determine understanding of the graphophonic system, they can note in specific detail the stages of development revealed by their students' invented spellings. Children's writing also seems particularly useful for determining insights they are acquiring beyond straight phoneme to grapheme mapping. When children begin to notice, as Paul did, (Bissix, 1980) that "if you take the L out of 'glass' and push it all together you get 'gas'," they have truly understood the alphabetic principle.

The following story about a trip to the zoo, written by a first grade boy, illustrates many of the concepts discussed above.

My favorite day in D-8 was
when we went to the zoo. fhrst
we got on the Bus sacnt we wr
on or way to the zoo thrd we wer
geting of the bus and we tok
or luchis. and we prt or lunches

My favorite day in D-8 was
when we went to the zoo. first
we got on the Bus second we were
on our way to the zoo third we were
getting off the Bus and we took
our lunches. and we put our lunches

Eeds

on the cort and then or techer tok	on the cart and then our teacher took
or lunches to the lunchroom.	our lunches to the lunchroom.
And when she got bak we whent	And when she got back we went
whith or group and we whent to see	with our group and we went to see
animals fhrst we whent to see	the animals first we went to see
the snacs and a chrachela	the snakes and a tarantula
and then we whent to the dazrt	and then we went to the desert
mazeum and we so the manliens	museum and we saw the mountain
and then we whent to see the	lions and then we went to see the
cheda But the cheda was in its	cheetah But the cheetah was in its
caga so we went to see the graf	cage so we went to see the giraffe
and we so a baby graf and we	and we saw a baby giraffe and we
so the Rinosrisis and there wher 2	saw the Rhinoceros and there were 2
Rinosrisis and we so thc lien	Rhinoceroses and we saw the lion
and then we whent to see the	and then we went to see the
pcocs and and the ciyodes and	peacocks and and the coyotes and
then we whent to the other animals.	then we went to the other animals.
and we so a popet sow and after	and we saw a puppet show and after
we so the popet sow	we saw the puppet show
we whent ;o pet the animals and	we went to pet the animals and
then we whent to see the Glopcis	then we went to see the Galapagos
todl and then we at lunch and then	turtle and then we ate lunch and then
we so a pcoc will we	we saw a peacock while we
were eating lunch	were eating lunch
we so 2 pecocs and we so the	we saw 2 peacocks and we saw the
spidr monces and we so the	spider monkeys and we saw the
ranatags and the we whent	orangutans and then we went
bac to the Bus and then we whent	back to the Bus and then we went
bac to scool.	back to school.

This child obviously has mastered directional principles. He knows where the print should go and is developing concepts of periods and capital letters. (Commas are not yet in evidence.) He retains some letter name strategies, as in *snacs* and *we at* lunch, but almost all of his invented spellings are phonetic and reflect considerable knowledge of the graphophonic system. It is possible to hypothesize about many of them. Is *saw* spelled *so* because he has been taught "short *o*"? Did he insert an *h* in *whent* and *fhrst* and *whith* because he is listening to his own pronunciations of the words as he writes (segmenting and recombining) and he hears an aspiration? Did he insert the *a* at the end of *caga* because he's aware there is something at the end (orthographic awareness), or does he hear *cage-uh* as he carefully pronounces the word?

This child's awareness that the intervocalic flap in *coyote* and cheetah is pronounced as a *d* is reflected in his spellings—*ciyode* and *cheda*. He hears the affricated sound of *t* and *r* together in *tarantula* and spells it *chrachela*. Vowels are not used in every word, but the developing awareness of them is clear. *Peacock* is spelled *pcoc* two times, but the last time he uses it he spells it *pecoc*. The exploration with variable consonants also can be seen. He spells *back* as *bac* and *bak,* but it can't be long before this child notices that both letters are required.

The examination of only a small portion of the writing that beginning readers should be doing daily is likely to yield rich insights into their hypotheses about the coding system. And it will provide rich materials for hypothesis making for the teacher as well.

Children's Oral Reading

As children begin to learn about written language in an environment that stresses meaning and is rich in providing information from which they can formulate hypotheses about how it all works (Goodman & Goodman, 1979; K. Goodman, 1986; Holdaway, 1979; Taylor, Blum, & Logsdon, 1986 for detailed descriptions of such environments), it is also possible to gain insight about their use of the coding system by listening to them read. Just as examining children's writing can provide clues about these developing hypotheses, K. Goodman (1979, p. 3) has noted that the miscues children make when they read are "windows into the mind" that allow the teacher to make predictions about the child's understanding of the coding system in the context of the other systems of language.

In 1972, Y. Goodman and Burke published the Reading Miscue Inventory (RMI), which was designed to help researchers, reading specialists, and teachers do a qualitative analysis rather than a quantitative assessment of children's oral reading miscues. This was very different from the conventional informal reading inventory that emphasized the reading of short paragraphs in test like situations, the counting of pronunciation errors, and the use of a few questions (often only tangentially related to the reading) to determine comprehension. The RMI and adaptations of it still appear to be the most meaningful way to assess developing mastery of the coding system (as only one of the systems used in reading). Differences between an expected response and an observed response are looked at in terms of how the reader is using graphic, phonological, syntactic, and semantic information in the pragmatic situation in which the reading is taking place. This means whole text is used (no fragments) that is long enough to allow the readers to use their language abilities and reading strategies. The oral reading and the retelling of the selection are taped, miscues are marked and analyzed, and a profile of reader strengths is prepared and used to plan a reading program.

Specific use of the coding system is looked at in the RMI or in adaptations of it (see Anderson, 1984; Cochrane et al., 1984 for detailed descriptions of these adaptations) by examining reader substitutions for actual words in the text. These substitutions are coded for graphic similiarity to the text word (do they look alike?) and phonological similarity (do they sound alike?) with judgments of *yes, some,* or *no.* An examination of at least twenty-five miscues can determine whether a reader is using the coding system to confirm predictions that also make sense syntactically and semantically. In the Cochrane et al. adaptation of the RMI, teachers ask four questions: Did the reader use graphophonics when s/he substituted this word for the word in the text? Does what the reader reads sound like language? Does what the reader reads make sense? Does the reader change the author's intended meaning?

Analysis of a reader's use of the coding system in the context of the others is extremely important. As Cochran et al. (1984, p. 25) noted, "If the use of one of the language cues is stressed over another, children will likely overuse that cue and neglect the other cues available to them." If a child substitutes *daddy* for *father* in her oral reading, her strength in using meaning and syntax to predict the expected word is to be celebrated and taken a step farther to help her use the coding system to confirm her predictions. If a child should say *feather* for *father,* however, a strength in using the coding system may be celebrated while the child is helped to use what she knows about meaning to make a more realistic prediction.

Although the original RMI was complicated and somewhat impractical for classroom use, a recent revision by Goodman, Watson, and Burke (1987) presents three alternatives to the original which make it practical for every classroom teacher. They give greatly simplified procedures for determining a child's mastery of the coding system in the context of the others.

To simplify even further, Holdaway (1979) has suggested that teachers regularly take running records of children's oral reading of texts they haven't seen before (perhaps keeping an audiotape for each child), mark their miscues as suggested in the RMI, and determine whether they are self-correcting as they read. This differs from the RMI in that no retelling is taken for comprehension assessment and no formal coding of miscues takes place, thus shortening the process considerably. He believes that children's ratio of self-corrections to total number of miscues is the "best index of healthy processing, and provides a clear idea of which children are having difficulty in developing sound central strategies" (p. 143). He cautions that children should read material in which they make no more than one (uncorrected) miscue in twenty words.

Summary

The use of nonsense words and tasks to test children's mastery of the coding system was not considered in this chapter, although it is common enough in practice. Careful observance of children's writing, close attention to what they say about their discoveries about print as they learn to write, and qualitative consideration of their miscues as they read whole text should give diagnosticians enough insight into children's use of both the orthographic and graphophonic aspects of the coding system to enable them to build on the considerable strengths that all children bring to the process of learning to read.

References

Anderson, G.S. *A whole language approach to reading.* Lanham, MD: University Press of America, 1984.

Beers, J.W., and Henderson, E.H. A study of developing orthographic concepts among first grade children. *Research in the Teaching of English,* 1977, *11,* 133-148.

Bissex, G.L. GNYS AT WRK: *A child learns to write and read.* Cambridge, MA: Harvard University Press, 1980.

Calkins, L.M. *The art of teaching writing.* Portsmouth, NH: Heinemann, 1986.

Chomsky, C. Approaching reading through invented spelling. In L.B. Resnick and P. Weaver (Eds.), *Theory and practice of early reading,* Volume 2. Hillsdale, NJ: Erlbaum, 1979, 43-65.

Clay, M.M. *Reading: The patterning of complex behavior.* Auckland, NZ: Heinemann, 1972.

Clay, M.M. *The early detection of reading difficulties.* Portsmouth, NH: Heinemann, 1979.

Cochrane, O., Cochrane, D., Scalena, S., and Buchanan, E. *Reading, writing, and caring.* New York: Richard C. Owen, 1984.

Ehri, L. Linguistic insight: Threshold of reading acquisition. In T. Waller and G.E. Mackinnon (Eds.), *Reading research: Advances in theory and practice,* volume 1. New York: Academic Press, 1979, 63-114.

Ehri, L., and Wilce, L. Does learning to spell help beginners learn to read words? *Reading Research Quarterly,* 1987, *21,* 47-65.

Ferreiro, E., and Teberosky, A. *Literacy before schooling.* Portsmouth, NH: Heinemann, 1982.

Flores, B.M., and Garcia, E.A. A collaborative learning and teaching experience using journal writing. *Journal for the National Association for Bilingual Education,* 1984, *8,* 67-83.

Gentry, J.R. An analysis of developmental spelling in GNYS AT WRK. *The Reading Teacher,* 1982, *36,* 192-200.

Gibson, E.J., and Levin, H. *The psychology of reading.* Cambridge, MA: MIT Press, 1975.

Goodman, K. *Miscue analysis: Applications to reading instruction.* Urbana, IL; National Council of Teachers of English, 1979.

Goodman, K. *What's whole about whole language?* Portsmouth, NH: Heinemann, 1986.

Goodman, K., and Goodman, Y. Learning to read is natural. In L. Resnick and P. Weaver (Eds.), *Theory and practice of early reading,* Volume 1. Hillsdale, NJ: Erlbaum, 1979, 137-154.

Goodman, Y. The development of initial literacy. In H. Goelman, A. Oberg, and F. Smith (Eds.), *Awakening to literacy.* London: Heinemann, 1984.

Goodman, Y., and Burke, C.L. *Reading miscue inventory: Procedures for diagnosis and evaluation.* New York: Macmillan, 1972.

Goodman, Y., Watson, D., and Burke, C. *Reading miscue inventory: Alternative procedures.* New York: Richard C. Owen, 1987.

Graves, D.H. *Writing: Teachers and children at work.* Portsmouth, NH: Heinemann, 1982.

Haddock, M. The effects of an auditory and an auditory-visual method of blending instruction on the ability of preschoolers to decode synthetic words. *Journal of Educational Psychology,* 1976, *68,* 825-831.

Haddock, M. Teaching blending in beginning reading is important. *The Reading Teacher,* 1978, *31,* 654-658.

Heath, S.B. What no bedtime story means: Narrative skills at home and school. *Language in Society,* 1982, *11,* 49-79.

Henderson, E.H., and Beers, J.W. (Eds.). *Developmental and cognitive aspects of learning to spell: A reflection of word knowledge.* Newark, DE: International Reading Association, 1980.

Holdaway, D. *The foundations of literacy.* Portsmouth, NH: Heinemann, 1979.

Liberman, I.Y., and Shankweiler, D. Phonology and the problems of learning to read and write. *Remedial and Special Education,* 1985, *6,* 8-17.

Lundberg, I. Longitudinal studies of reading and reading difficulties in Sweden. In G.E. MacKinnon and T.E. Waller (Eds.), *Reading research: Advances in theory and practice,* Volume 4. New York: Academic Press, 65-103.

Morris, D. Concept of a word: A developmental phenomenon. In J. Jensen (Ed), *Composing and comprehending.* Urbana, IL: National Conference on Research in English, 1984.

Olson, R.K., Kliegl, R., Davidson, B.J., and Foltz, G. Individual and developmental differences in reading disability. In G.E. MacKinnon and T.G. Waller (Eds.), *Reading research: Advances in theory and practice,* Volume 4. New York: Academic Press, 1984.

Perfetti, C.A. Reading acquisition and beyond: Decoding includes cognition. *American Journal of Education,* 1984, *93,* 40-60.

Read, C. *Children's categorizations of speech sounds in English.* Urbana, IL: National Council of Teachers of English, 1975.

Resnick, L.B. Theories and prescriptions for early reading instruction. In L. Resnick and P. Weaver (Eds.), *Theory and practice of early reading,* Volume 1. Hillsdale, NJ: Erlbaum, 1979, 321-338.

Taylor, N.E., Blum, I.H., and Logsdon, D.M. The development of written language awareness: Environmental aspects and program characteristics. *Reading Research Quarterly,* 1986, *21,* 132-149.

Wallach, M., and Wallach, L. Helping disadvantaged children learn to read by teaching them phoneme identification skills. In L.B. Resnick and P. Weaver (Eds.), *Theory and practice of early reading,* Volume 3. Hillsdale, NJ: Erlbaum, 1979, 197-215.

John E. Readence
Michael A. Martin

5

Comprehension Assessment: Alternatives to Standardized Tests

W hen we discuss the topic of assessment (the use of standard-ized reading comprehension tests in particular) teachers ask "Which standardized test would you recommend our school district use?" The major point we stress is that the primary concern about a reading comprehension assessment measure is the degree to which it represents *real* reading tasks and situations. In our judgment, standardized reading comprehension tests are not representative of the reading tasks students are assigned in the classroom. In fact, Johnston (1984, p. 169) alluded to the notion that much of what we currently do in the name of reading comprehension assessment can be characterized as strange or abnormal.

In this chapter we trace the historical development of stand-ardized reading comprehension tests to show they were developed for the sake of convenience in test construction and scoring rather than for diagnostic information. We will make a case for the use of informal measures of reading comprehension; discuss the use of in-formal measures such as miscue analysis and the content reading inventory; and describe the role of *observation* as a means of read-ing comprehension assessment, providing examples of its use. The purpose of this chapter is to provide teachers with alternatives to consider in gathering diagnostic information about their students' comprehension instructional needs.

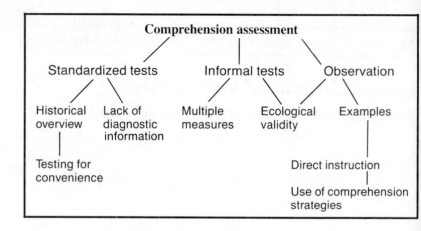

Why Questions?

The purpose of standardized reading comprehension tests is to compare performances of various groups of students at a particular grade level. In this way, school districts can see how their students compare nationally and can make decisions about the quality of the instructional program offered.

The typical standardized reading comprehension test format, however, consists of reading short paragraphs and answering accompanying multiple choice questions. Such a format provides a limited measure of how well students comprehend text (e.g., Farr & Carey, 1986). Choosing appropriate answers to questions is just one indicator of reading comprehension. Students can show they have understood a text by producing miscues, retelling passages, or dramatizing stories.

Students restricted to answering questions do not have an opportunity to display other important comprehending behaviors. For instance, students are not able to demonstrate their ability to pose questions, justify their answers, or anticipate what is coming in the text. Given these limitations, why do questions predominate as the format used in standardized reading comprehension tests? In an examination of the literature from the early years of this century, Readence and Moore (1983) illustrated how early test designers concentrated on objective and convenient measures of comprehension at the expense of providing a more complete picture of students' comprehending abilities and how this led to the predominant use of questions today.

Three types of comprehension test formats emerged from this examination: reproducing a passage, solving written puzzles, and answering questions. Passage reproduction was advocated by Starch, who felt that comprehension should be determined by the most simple, rapid, and objective means possible and suggested that a count of the written words that correctly express the thought of a passage would accomplish this. He asked students to read passages on two consecutive days and to recall what they had read. Comprehension was determined by "counting the number of words written which correctly reproduce the thought. The written account is carefully read, and all words which either reproduce the ideas of the test passage incorrectly or add ideas not in the test passage or repeat ideas previously recorded are crossed out. The remaining words are counted and used as the index of comprehension" (Starch, 1915, p. 7).

The phrase "correctly reproduce the thought" unfortunately meant verbatim reproduction to Starch. Thus, comprehension was measured by students' ability to recall a passage exactly; inferences and synonym substitutions were discounted.

Although Starch felt his test was simple, rapid, and objective, other researchers did not. Reproducing a passage was criticized as impractical due to the time involved in scoring (Kallom, 1920), invalid because of low correlations to other measures of comprehension (Gates, 1921), and inappropriate because there was a question as to whether this task actually reflected students' abilities to comprehend that passage (Monroe, DeVoss, & Kelly, 1917).

In response to the objections to the reproduction format, Kelly (1916) developed the Kansas Reading Test that required simple responses to short paragraphs. Students were given five minutes to respond to sixteen exercises at the appropriate test level. Below are two sample test items from the test for grades three through five.

3. Three words are given below. One of them has been left out of the sentence: I cannot _____ the girl who has

the flag. Draw a line around the word which is needed in
the above sentence.

red   see   come

16. If in the following words *e* comes right after *a* more
times than *e* comes just after *i*, then put a line under
each word containing an *e* and an *i*, but if *e* comes just
before *a* more often than right after *i*, then put a line
under each word containing an *a* and an *e*.

receive   feather
teacher   believe

This test format required reasoning similar to that of solving
puzzles and demanded that students follow directions exactly. For
instance, if in the first example, the student underlined (and did not
circle) the correct response "see," the exercise would be counted as
incorrect — comprehension failure was assumed.

This puzzle format was criticized by researchers of the day.
Starch (1916) and Monroe, DeVoss, and Kelly (1917) felt the tasks
assessed only a narrow band of comprehending behavior and did not
represent normal reading situations. Gray (1917) said puzzle formats did not allow for varying degrees of comprehension; he felt it
unjust to mark something incorrect when it was obvious the student
understood the task but did not follow directions explicitly.

The third major comprehension test format was proposed by
Thorndike (1914, p. 207), who saw the need for "more objective,
more accurate, and more convenient measures of . . . a pupil's ability to understand the meaning of words and sentences seen." To this
end, Thorndike developed the Scale Alpha, which consisted of a series of short paragraphs and questions of increasing difficulty. Students were asked to read the passages and write answers to the
questions that accompanied them. No time limit was imposed.

Following is an example of a paragraph and its questions
from Scale Alpha (pp. 251-252). As you will note, question four is
closely akin to the word puzzle format and has nothing to do with
the paragraph.

Set C

Read this and then write the answers. Read it again as often
as you need to.

It may seem at first thought that every boy and girl who goes to school ought to do all the work the teacher wishes done. But sometimes other duties prevent even the best boy or girl from doing so. If a boy's or girl's father died and he had to work afternoons and evenings to earn money to help his mother, such might be the case. A good girl might let her lessons go undone in order to help her mother by taking care of the baby.

1. What are some conditions that might even make the best boy leave school work unfinished?
2. What might a boy do in the evenings to help his family?
3. How could a girl be of use to her mother?
4. Look at these words: idle tribe inch it ice ivy tide true tip top tit tat toe. Cross out every one of them that has an *i* and has not any *t* in it.

Gray (1917, p. 7) observed that "the scale fulfills the standards of objectivity, definiteness, exactitude, and convenience." This format could be given and scored quickly and impartially, overcoming many of the objections of the reproduction and puzzle formats.

The question format was not without its detractors. In the same writing, Gray pointed out that the test measured only a limited aspect of students' ability to comprehend text. Shank (1930, p. 129) stated that tests employing the question format asked the student to "write his response to a question whose answer may be found directly in the content." Tuinman (1973) pointed out that questions may not be passage dependent; students might be able to answer the questions without reading the passage. Thus, it can be surmised that this format does not always measure students' true comprehending abilities.

By 1930 the question format became the predominant means of assessing comprehension and the prototype for current standardized tests of reading comprehension. Educators felt that answering questions offered the most convenient, economical, and objective format for comprehension assessment. The popularity of this format was further enhanced by the fact that questions were adaptable to the multiple choice formats popular in the 1930s and to computerized scoring in the 1960s.

Yet, the question format does represent a compromise on the part of educators. In gaining convenience and objectivity, educators gave up obtaining a more complete picture of students' comprehending abilities. Numerous educators feel that students' ability to comprehend is multifaceted and that reliance on a single measure of this complex construct is unwarranted (Carroll, 1972; Dewey, 1934; Petrosky, 1982; Pressey & Pressey, 1921).

Standardized reading comprehension tests may help sort students and compare groups according to rough measures of general academic abilities, but these tests provide only limited information about the specific comprehending abilities of students. As a result there is not sufficient diagnostic information to allow teachers to plan instruction. Teachers require the results of other informal and observational measures of comprehension to obtain more complete pictures of students' comprehension abilities and to use that information to plan for appropriate instruction.

Informal Comprehension Measures

Since comprehension is essentially an internal, unobservable phenomenon, we can gauge only behaviors that reflect it. Thus, the more methods used, the better the chance teachers have of making valid assessments (Johnston, 1984). While there are numerous informal measures that can be used to build a picture of students' comprehending abilities, we advocate the use of measures relevant to what students are reading and learning about in their classrooms; i.e., ecologically valid measures of students as they are interacting with relevant reading tasks and situations in their basal readers and content textbooks.

While we acknowledge that additional diagnostic information can be gained about students' comprehending abilities through other assessment measures—such as a published informal reading inventory—the reading tasks students are asked to perform deal with contrived text and not with naturally occurring text used daily in classroom reading assignments. We would recommend that if teachers were to use an informal reading inventory to gather the most relevant diagnostic information possible, the inventory should be designed to use passages from the textbooks students use.

While we have stated that a question format does assess only limited aspects of students' comprehension, questions can help gather a more complete picture of their abilities. Questions can be designed to examine how well students can cope with the new vocabulary of a textbook, to examine how well students can internalize the ideas of the basal or textbook by asking questions that go beyond the facts stated in them (i.e., questions at the text implicit or experience based levels of comprehension), and to see how well students cope with the various book parts (e.g., table of contents, index) available to aid them in the reading/learning process.

Teachers can then go beyond what they learn from asking questions by engaging students in other types of assessment measures. For example, students can be asked to read orally a passage from their textbook, and teachers can examine the miscues students make as they try to understand what they read. In this way, miscues provide an ongoing process measure that goes beyond questions and asks "*Is* the student comprehending?" rather than "*What* is the student comprehending?" (Allen & Watson, 1976). Students could be asked to react in writing to a narrative passage to see whether they are attending mainly to surface level plot structures, character development, or underlying universal themes (Purves, 1968). The above mentioned measures of comprehension, plus those mentioned earlier in this chapter as alternatives to asking questions, are all appropriate for obtaining more complete pictures of students' abilities to understand what they read. The next section of this chapter adds more information to those pictures.

Diagnosis by Observation

Most traditional forms of assessment measure a student's performance at that point in time only. Additionally, the administration of traditional assessment measures on a one time basis does not provide sufficient information for drawing conclusions about students' abilities because (as previously discussed) most focus on a narrow set of comprehending behaviors. Teachers need additional information gained from multiple measures administered periodically to obtain updated information. This does not mean administering more of the same types of tests; it requires teachers to be more sensitive to the entire instructional situation and the major variables involved in it. Teachers need to be concerned with the reader, the text, the task required of the reader, and the actual processes needed to complete the task (Readence, Bean, & Baldwin, 1985). Assessment needs to be conducted as students interact with text and complete daily classroom assignments.

Actual classroom reading assignments can provide many good sources of diagnostic information that cannot be gained through traditional assessment. Specifically, teachers need to make a conscious effort to observe and study their students at work in several classroom settings (see Glazer & Searfoss, this volume). Moore (1983) referred to this as *naturalistic assessment* because it requires teachers to observe students' responses to naturally occurring classroom activities instead of to more contrived testing situations. Teachers observe students as they participate in a variety of circumstances over a period of time and try to identify patterns of behavior that may represent difficulty in some area. These patterns are then interpreted and used to reach conclusions regarding students' strengths and weaknesses. This information then can be added to and compared with that gained from more traditional assessment devices.

Naturalistic procedures, or observations, may be the most valid and reliable means of assessing reading comprehension (Moore, 1983). Their validity is strong because daily observations occur as a natural part of the lesson; teachers view students' responses in an objective, unbiased manner; and the observations are conducted in the natural context of real reading (Cunningham, 1982). This allows the teacher to assess what students have learned and to observe how well students apply what they have learned as they read.

High reliability is achieved because of the nature of observational assessment. Specifically, because teachers base their conclusions on numerous observations over a period of time, they avoid an essential problem of more traditional assessment measures—lack of consistency. The observed patterns that lead to the conclusions are patterns that have occurred frequently in real reading situations and not in contrived testing situations. Finally, observations are planned, structured, and systematic (Cunningham, 1982).

The use of observations as a means of comprehension assessment presents a viable alternative to traditional assessment devices. The most important aspect of this approach revolves around the idea that assessment is ongoing and conducted within the context of normal classroom activities while real reading is taking place. We will now present a model of direct instruction in which the use of observational assessment can be integrated and discuss examples of some specific strategies that lend themselves to this type of assessment.

Direct Instruction. During the late 1960s and the 1970s, developmental psychologists investigated possible effects of instructional intervention upon reading comprehension. As a result, numerous research studies in the late 1970s and early 1980s were conducted for the specific purpose of determining the instructional characteristics of effective reading comprehension instruction. The question governing these pursuits was, "Can students be made aware of reading comprehension strategies or be taught skills that would transfer to independent reading situations?" (Tierney, Readence, & Dishner, 1985, p. 84). The concept of explicit teaching of reading comprehension, or direct instruction, emerged from these research studies.

The features constituting direct instruction have been addressed by numerous researchers of reading comprehension (e.g., Palincsar & Brown, 1983; Pearson & Gallagher, 1983; Tierney & Cunningham, 1984). In their 1985 text, Tierney, Readence, and Dishner (1985, p. 85) described those features in the following manner:

1. *Relevance.* Students are made aware of the purpose of the skill or strategy.
2. *Definition.* Students are informed as to how to apply the skills by making public the skill or strategy.
3. *Guided Practice.* Students are given feedback on their own use of the skill or strategy.
4. *Self-regulation.* Students are given opportunities to try out the strategy themselves and develop ways to monitor their own use of the skill or strategy.
5. *Gradual Release of Responsibility.* The teacher initially models and directs the students' learning. As the lesson

progresses, the teacher gradually gives more responsibility to the students.

6. *Application.* Students are given the opportunity to try their skills and strategies in independent learning situations, including nonschool tasks.

Additionally, the implementation of a direct instruction lesson calls for teachers to follow certain guidelines that help them assimilate the important features of direct instruction into the lesson. What follows is a presentation of the specific guidelines and examples of possible questions/statements teachers could use if they were attempting to teach main idea comprehension in a family living class.

1. Introduce the skill or strategy by providing examples of what you are teaching and by relating the examples to the students' prior knowledge. In addition to tapping prior knowledge, this step also establishes the purpose of the strategy. For example, asking the following would be useful: "Have you ever been on a blind date? How did you find out what the person you were dating was like? Imagine you have gotten a friend a blind date. You have to tell your friend the most important features of the person she or he will be going out with. How would you do this?"

2. The next stage involves teachers in labeling, modeling, defining, and explaining the skill or strategy. The how, when, and where of the strategy is presented through negative and positive examples. For example, teachers explain that students are going to learn more about main ideas. The students are instructed to read a story in which Bob is telling Dave about the blind date he has for the Spring Formal. Afterwards, teachers discuss how they would select the main idea and important facts in the story.

3. The teacher and students read through another example story to provide guided practice. For example, a story to find out about Mike's blind date for the Spring Formal.

4. Students are provided independent practice through the use of a checklist or reading guide. For example they read a story to find out about Sally's blind date for the Spring

Formal and to decide whether the main idea of Sally's story is what Sally does on her date, what Sally's blind date wants to do on their date, or what Sally's blind date is really like. Advise students to identify the most important facts and ideas. Students discuss their decisions.

5. The final stage involves independent application by the students. For example, the teacher suggests the students apply their skills/strategies to a fourth story about Bill's experiences with his blind date at the Spring Formal. After a discussion of this application, students give examples of how they could use this skill in other classes.

Through the application of direct instruction, students will learn how to independently apply the skills/strategies identified as essential to successful comprehension. In addition, teachers are able to teach these specific skills/strategies through direct instruction and, as teaching occurs, are able to successfully assess (through observation) their students' learning. For instance, in this lesson, teachers can observe whether students grasp the purpose of getting the main idea of a passage; understand how to get the main idea; can apply what they have been taught before and after reteaching; are able to verbalize their thinking about how they derived the main idea; and can independently derive main ideas from other texts.

Specific Comprehension Strategies. As stated earlier, one of the benefits of observational assessment is that assessment occurs as students are involved with instructional activities in the actual context of their classrooms. Through the use of a direct instruction approach, teachers are able to observe their students' applications of skills/strategies. However, there are additional comprehension strategies that lend themselves to observational assessment. In this section, the anticipation guide and the guided reading procedure will be discussed.

Anticipation Guides. An anticipation guide (Readence, Bean, & Baldwin, 1985) attempts to enhance students' comprehension through the activation of their prior knowledge. Through the use of controversial statements, students are motivated to become involved with the material they are about to read.

Anticipation guides can be used as an assessment measure. As students react to the statements, teachers can observe how much students know about a topic. The guides also allow teachers to observe how well students interact with one another as they attempt to make predictions concerning a topic. Teachers can observe how well students pose their own questions, anticipate what is to come in the text, and justify their responses to guide statements. Finally, teachers can observe how well students recognize and reconcile prior knowledge inaccuracies when they encounter them in reading.

Guided Reading Procedure (GRP). The GRP was developed by Manzo (1975) to provide teachers with a series of instructional steps that would assist students with material being read in the classroom. Specifically, the GRP was designed to assist students' recall of information, improve students' abilities to create their own implicit questions during reading, develop students' understanding of the importance of self-correction, and improve students' abilities to organize information (Tierney, Readence, & Dishner, 1985).

As teachers guide their students through the various stages of the GRP, they can observe their interactions with the material. Teachers can observe and judge the quality of their students' recall of information after reading. For those students who need additional assistance in this area, teachers can refocus attention on missing information and students' efforts to ask questions to fill in gaps in recall. Additionally, it can be noted which students have trouble organizing the recalls, and further instruction can be planned to deal with these problems.

Summary

In this chapter we have traced the development of standardized reading comprehension tests to demonstrate that obtaining a more complete picture of students' comprehending abilities has been sacrificed for the sake of convenience and objectivity. Because little useful diagnostic information can be attained from these measures, teachers need alternative measures of students' abilities. We have recommended that this information be obtained by using more ecologically valid measures of comprehension. Discussions have been provided of possible informal measures of comprehension that can give teachers multiple sources of information. The additional use of observation by teachers as they interact with their students can be very helpful in developing more complete pictures of students' comprehending abilities. Finally, examples were provided of the kinds of diagnostic information teachers can obtain through observation when in the actual course of comprehension instruction. It is our hope the information provided here will do what we had intended — provide teachers with some viable and useful alternatives in reading comprehension assessment.

References

Allen, P.D., and Watson, D.J. (Eds.) *Findings of research in miscue analysis: Classroom implications.* Champaign, IL: ERIC/RCS and National Council of Teachers of English, 1976.

Carroll, J.B. Defining language comprehension: Some speculations. In R. Freedle and J.B. Carroll (Eds.), *Language comprehension and the acquisition of knowledge.* New York: Halstead (Division of Wiley), 1972, 1-29.

Cunningham, P.M. Diagnosis by observation. In J.J. Pikulski and T. Shanahan (Eds.), *Approaches to the informal evaluation of reading.* Newark, DE: International Reading Association, 1982.

Dewey, J.C. A technique for investigating reading comprehension. *School and Society,* 1934, *39,* 276.

Farr, R., and Carey, R.F. *Reading: What can be measured?* second edition. Newark, DE: International Reading Association, 1986.

Gates, A.I. An experimental and statistical study of reading and reading tests. *Journal of Educational Psychology,* 1921, *12,* 303-314, 378-391, 445-464.

Gray, W.S. *Studies of elementary school reading through standardized tests.* Supplementary Educational Monographs, No. 1. Chicago: University of Chicago Press, 1917.

Johnston, P.H. Assessment in reading. In P.D. Pearson (Ed.), *Handbook of reading research.* New York: Longman, 1984.

Kallom, A.W. Reproduction as a measure of reading ability. *Journal of Educational Research,* 1920, *1,* 359-368.

Kelly, F.J. The Kansas silent reading tests. *Journal of Educational Psychology,* 1916, *7,* 63-80.

Manzo, A.V. Guided reading procedure. *Journal of Reading,* 1975, *18,* 287-291.

Monroe, W.S., DeVoss, J.C., and Kelly, F.J. *Educational tests and measurements.* Boston: Houghton Mifflin, 1917.

Moore, D.W. A case for naturalistic assessment of reading comprehension. *Language arts,* 1983, *60,* 957-969.

Palincsar, A., and Brown, A. *Reciprocal teaching of comprehension monitoring activities,* Technical Report No. 269. Champaign, IL: University of Illinois, Center for the Study of Reading, 1983.

Pearson, P.D., and Gallagher, M.C. The instruction of reading comprehension. *Contemporary Educational Psychology,* 1983, *8,* 317-344.

Petrosky, A.R. From story to essay: Reading and writing. *College Composition and Communication,* 1982, *33,* 19-36.

Pressey, L.W., and Pressey, S.L. A critical study of the concept of silent reading ability. *Journal of Educational Psychology,* 1921, *12,* 25-31.

Purves, A.C. *Elements of writing about a literary work.* Champaign, IL: National Council of Teachers of English, 1968.

Readence, J.E., Bean, T.W., and Baldwin, R.S. *Content area reading: An integrated approach,* second edition. Dubuque, IA: Kendall/Hunt, 1985.

Readence, J.E., and Moore, D.W. Why questions? A historical perspective on standardized reading comprehension tests. *Journal of Reading,* 1983, *26,* 306-313.

Shank, S. Student responses in the measurement of reading comprehension. *Journal of Educational Research,* 1930, *22,* 119-129.

Starch, D. The measurement of efficiency in reading. *Journal of Educational Psychology,* 1915, *6,* 1-24.

Starch, D. *Educational measurements.* New York: Macmillan, 1916.

Thorndike, E.L. The measurement of ability in reading. *Teachers College Record,* 1914, *15,* 207-277.

Tierney, R.J., and Cunningham, J.W. Research on teaching reading comprehension. In P.D. Pearson (Ed.), *Handbook on reading research.* New York: Longman, 1984.

Tierney, R.J., Readence, J.E., and Dishner, E.K. *Reading strategies and practices: A compendium,* second edition. Boston: Allyn & Bacon, 1985.

Tuinman, J.J. Determining the passage dependency of comprehension questions in five major tests. *Reading Research Quarterly,* 1973, *9,* 206-223.

Readence and Martin

Measuring Comprehension: Alternative Diagnostic Approaches

T his chapter describes informal procedures that can be used to diagnose the abilities of students to recall information derived from print. The methods presented are alternatives to the traditional question-answer format. Strategies are presented to help students organize for more effective recall as well as provide ongoing diagnostic information for the teacher. Factors are discussed that affect students' understanding of text and their ability to assimilate new information into existing schemata.

Case studies of disabled readers are replete with test results and anecdotal records that report the difficulty these students have remembering information they have read. The causes for their limited recall often are not ascertained; consequently, the instruction they receive in classrooms and resource rooms may not address deficit areas. Instead, traditional teaching procedures that focus on reading and questioning are followed. Teachers may adhere to this conventional method because school records lack specificity in identifying academic deficits. Both formal and informal test results can mask weaknesses in comprehending and recalling written text. Although students may attain similar achievement levels on a test, there may be significant differences in their abilities to organize and freely recall information contained in reading selections. Students of all ages must learn to assimilate new knowledge in a classification system and recall it without the aid of teacher generated questions. Assessments of reading competency should include procedures that

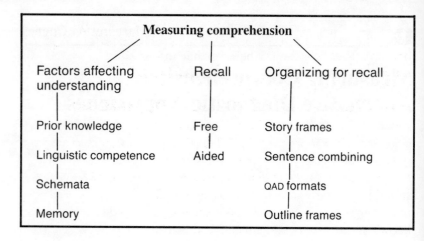

will yield information about recall without the aid of questions, along with specifics about the structure of the recall.

Major Factors Affecting Comprehension

The assessment of comprehension demands an awareness of various elements that contribute to effective understanding of written text, including prior knowledge, linguistic competence, memory, and schemata. Each plays a crucial role in the way readers comprehend printed materials and organize important ideas so they can be retrieved at another time.

According to Johnston and Pearson (1982), prior knowledge influences the comprehension process at all levels. It aids the reader in selecting words that will fit the context of a sentence, determines the amount of information that can be stored in both short term and long term memory, decides the form in which it will be stored, and plays a decisive role in helping an individual make inferences.

Studies have shown that linguistic competence is related to successful reading (Edmiaston, 1985; Laine, 1978). Students must have language labels for experiences so they can expand their vocabularies and better understand written text. The syntax of reading selections should be familiar to them so understanding is facilitated. Furthermore, they must be able to combine sounds into words. All of these linguistic factors contribute to successful reading.

Cagney

Teachers are aware of the role memory plays in the comprehension process. Prior knowledge rests on the endurance of memory. Many psychologists believe that information is stored and retrieved on the basis of meaning (Baron, Byrne, & Kantowitz, 1977). In other words, knowledge is assimilated in one's memory in some type of organized structure governed by meaningful categorization. Readers have stored in long term memory general knowledge about the world and knowledge specific to their lives. Both types of knowledge affect their comprehension of textual material.

Schema theory attempts to explain the way that knowledge is stored in memory. Information about a particular topic is organized in a cognitive framework called a schema. Each schema represents knowledge of a particular concept and is related to other schemata in the hierarchy. Theorists believe the interrelationships among schemata help readers understand written text and affect the way material is recalled from memory (Adams & Collins, 1985). Rumelhart (1984) suggests that readers may fail to comprehend because they do not have appropriate schemata, the author may not have provided sufficient clues to suggest a specific schema, or the reader and writer might not share the same schemata.

When evaluating students' performances on tests or in diagnostic activities, the influence of their experiential backgrounds should be considered. Language variables, within the reader and within the text, need to be examined when learners have difficulty comprehending. Furthermore, the type of memory demanded in an assessment should be noted. Since information is stored and retrieved on the basis of meaning, an understanding of schema theory may help a teacher design informal procedures that evaluate retention of concepts over a period of time. The rest of this chapter will describe procedures that can be used to evaluate student's abilities to organize and retain important information in ongoing diagnostic teaching.

Assessing Recall of Written Information

Most individually administered reading tests require students to answer questions after reading a paragraph orally or silently. An instructional level is ascertained based on the number of correct responses and the number of words pronounced accurately. Directed reading lessons also follow a question-answer format. The main benefit derived from using this procedure is a major limitation in assessing and developing comprehension skills. Asking questions helps students remember significant ideas and details; however, almost every day we must recall information gained through print without the aid of questions. Thus, conclusions about an individual's reading ability based solely on postreading questions could be misleading and minimally helpful in planning relevant instruction. A diagnostic procedure that combines free and aided recall might more accurately evaluate comprehension ability.

The case studies of two boys, Steven and Jerry, clearly illustrate the limitations inherent in traditional evaluation procedures. School records based on informal reading inventories indicated that the boys' achievement levels in reading were similar. Scores used to determine the levels were based on responses to questions asked after reading (aided recall). When reading orally, Steven hesitated frequently and mispronounced and repeated words; mispronunciation errors were usually detected and corrected. In contrast, Jerry was a fluent oral reader and was being instructed at a higher level than Steven. Teachers were puzzled by the boys' responses to instruction. Steven usually provided more accurate and thoughtful responses in both reading and content subject lessons. Testing helped to explain some of the incongruities teachers found perplexing. By first assessing each boy's retelling ability (unaided recall) and then asking questions, teachers obtained a more exact description of their competencies. Figure 1 presents the comprehension scores the boys attained after reading a paragraph at the third grade reading level.

At this level and all others, Steven's retellings were more inclusive and more accurately sequenced than Jerry's. However, when questions were used to help the boys remember details from the paragraphs, their scores were remarkably similar. A comparison between these two aspects of comprehension pointed out the necessity for teaching Jerry strategies that might develop his ability to recall more of the important content and sequence.

Retelling has been used as an assessment tool in many research studies (Gambrell, Pfeiffer, & Wilson, 1985; Irwin & Mitch-

Figure 1
Jerry's and Steven's Comprehension Scores

Jerry		Steven	
Unaided	Aided	Unaided	Aided
+(2)		+(1)	
	+	+(2)	
+(1)		+(3)	
	+	+(4)	
	−	+(5)	
+(3)		+(6)	
+(4)		+(7)	
	+	+(8)	
	+		+
+(5)		+(9)	
90%		100%	

ell, 1983; Stein & Glenn, 1979). Irwin and Mitchell found flaws in a strictly quantitative analysis of retellings and suggested attention be given to both quantitative and qualitative analyses. Thus, when retelling is used for assessment purposes or for instruction, teachers should identify important elements in narrative or expository selections before asking students to read them. Then, during the retelling, teachers can readily determine the extent to which students can recall important details. As a postretelling activity, teachers can ask questions to elicit details not included in the retelling. The questions may draw attention to certain story elements that are consistently overlooked by readers and indicate an area for instruction. So, retelling can be simultaneously a diagnostic technique and an instructional method.

Depending upon the ages and abilities of students, details may be recalled orally or in writing. Reading important points either in words or phrases seems to help many disabled readers recall information in sequence, besides providing graphic evidence of

Figure 2
Percentages of Important Details Recalled

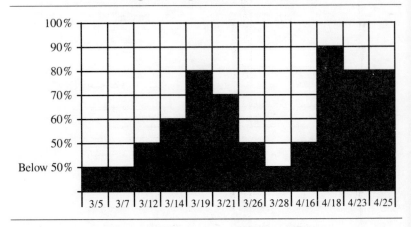

achievement. The number of details remembered may be noted on a cumulative chart used over a period of time; thus, some students observe that progress is steady and consistent while others become aware of the peaks and valleys in their learning pattern. One ten year old boy likened the charting of memories to keeping score in a sporting activity, so it was highly motivational. His chart reflected inconsistency (Figure 2) and prompted him to say, "Sometimes I do good and the next time I don't."

Assessing Organization for Recall

Reading achievement may be evaluated in a single session or over a period of time. Although the latter is more desirable, sometimes circumstances dictate testing in one session. The diagnostic findings from such a session are tentative, and competencies may change. Thus, ongoing diagnostic teaching, based on recommendations, becomes an avenue for further evaluation (Glazer & Searfoss, 1988). Insights into students' strengths and needs come with each new lesson. This continuous flow of information enriches the evaluation process and makes it more accurate.

Figure 3
Story Frame for Plot

In this story the problem starts when _____ . After that,
_____ . Next, _____ .
Then, _____ . The problem is
finally solved when _____ . The story ends _____
_____ .

Instructional strategies can provide guidance in recalling and organizing information and also yield evaluative data. Understanding and recall of text can be assessed by examining the way a story or outline frame is completed. Sentence combining exercises provide insights into language proficiency at the sentence and paragraph levels. Formats such as question-answer-details and outline frames test organizational skills and the ability to perceive relationships between important ideas and supporting details. The rest of this chapter focuses on the use of story frames, sentence combining, QAD formats, and outline frames in ongoing diagnostic teaching.

Story Frames

A story frame is a series of spaces linked by key language elements that often are transition words and reflect a particular line of thought. A frame may refer to the plot, setting, theme, or characters of a story. After reading a story, students complete a frame about it. Figure 3 illustrates a frame relating to the plot of a story.

According to Nichols (1980) and Fowler (1982), story frames provide a structure that helps low achieving readers organize information so they can identify important points, analyze characters and their problems, make comparisons, and summarize the content of passages. Frames are particularly helpful for students who are not proficient in writing.

Story frames can provide insights about oral and silent reading ability, memory for details, prior knowledge, and understanding of syntax. Some disabled readers may need to reread parts of a story orally in order to complete a frame. The teacher may have to direct students' attention in the story to specific sentences that supply information required for a response. At first, use stories that are easy and of interest to the reader. Over a period of time, however, oral rereading as well as specific directions from the teacher should be eliminated and the reading level of the story increased.

Analysis of a completed frame can furnish information about prior knowledge and the extent to which it enhances understanding or acts as a deterent to it. A student who was an avid television viewer often used knowledge gained from this medium to camouflage his inability to recall information. The deception became apparent when he completed modified story frames constructed for expository reading selections. Inadequate comprehension skills often are not detected in the elementary grades; students' experiential backgrounds help them to make reasonable, but not accurate, responses to postreading questions.

A reader's syntactical knowledge can be assessed in a limited way by using story frames. Students must understand and be able to produce basic sentence patterns as well as those that have been altered and expanded by clauses and phrases. Continuous observation may reveal deficiencies in specific areas. For one student, it was clear after completing four or five frames that she did not produce complete prepositional phrases. For instance, she would write "Some animals live on land and others live in sea." Examination of story frames led to the recognition of this deficiency in both written and oral language.

Through careful scrutiny of a few story frames, teachers and diagnosticians can discover instructional needs that might not appear in traditional testing situations. The frames that yield these diagnostic insights also help readers understand and organize information.

Sentence Combining

Sentence combining is a technique frequently used to increase syntactic fluency in writing. At first, students are taught to combine simple kernel sentences into a fairly simple sentence. Later, they learn to make more complex combinations. Lefevre (1970) believes that reading comprehension can be improved when the sentence is emphasized as the basic meaning bearing unit instead of the word. Research conducted by Frose and Kurushima (1979) supports the value of teaching sentence combining. They found that the abilities of third grade children to understand syntactically complex sentences improved after receiving instruction in this technique. Neville and Searls (1985) found that sentence combining and kernel identification exercises helped sixth grade students to recall syntactically complex text. Strong (1976) suggests that sentence combining is a powerful approach because it teaches students to retain longer discourse in their memories.

When readers have difficulty comprehending written language, their understanding of sentences should be assessed. Exercises in sentence combining may be both diagnostic and instructional. Students can be presented with two kernel sentences and told to merge them into one. Being able to read the sentences but not able to combine them may be an indication that expanded sentences are not part of their oral language. Instruction probably should focus on developing this skill. Frose and Kurushima found that students understood passages written at their productive language level but had difficulty comprehending above that level.

Evaluation should not be limited to combining two kernel sentences. Intermediate and secondary level textbooks require understanding of complex sentences. Thus, ability to combine expanded sentences and to use conjunctions and pronouns should be assessed. Given a list of pronouns, students might be asked to combine "She looked at the boy" with "The boy came out of the gray house."

Educators generally agree that productive language ability is basic to reading comprehension. However, children tend to be mysterious, unpredictable creatures. One boy could recall most of the important points in a reading selection despite the fact that his oral expression was restricted. When tested, he was unable to combine simple sentences. After a few instructional sessions, he understood the procedure for merging two or three closely related kernel sentences. Ongoing diagnostic teaching showed a need for further instruction in producing more complex sentences. So a single lesson in sentence combining may reveal important language deficiencies, even when comprehension is satisfactory.

Figure 4
QAD Chart

Question	Answer	Detail
What do we call the place that is the farthest north on earth?	*North Pole*	*where all the north and south lines come together at the top.*
What would you find at this place?	*a big sheet of snow*	*the sea is covered with ice no pole*
Who was the first person to reach this place?	*Matthew Henson*	*he is an explorer he is a blackman*

QAD *Formats*

Question-answer-detail charts require students to provide details that support their answers to specific questions. In preparing a QAD, students formulate questions about important points in a story. After reading the selection, students write answers to the questions along with supporting details, without referring to the story. Figure 4 presents an example of a QAD chart. This technique has been used successfully in schools that employ the Individualized Language Arts Program (1974).

An inability to answer questions on a QAD chart can indicate inadequate retention. Responses may be logical but derived from experiences rather than from the story. Some readers will answer questions quickly and accurately but have difficulty supplying details; they are unable to justify their responses. Since the purpose of a QAD is to elicit replies congruent with the text, students may need to refer to the story in order to complete the chart. A teacher may have to ask probing questions to guide their thinking. However, the main reason for using QAD strategy is to help students organize information and develop retention; thus, they should be weaned from the practice of referring to the story.

QAD formats provide diagnostic data about students' comprehension, retention, and understanding of relationships among details in a story. The charts provide an organizational structure that facilitates recall. According to schema theory, this type of structure is necessary for the storage and retrieval of information (Adams & Collins, 1986). Additionally, the technique fosters metacognitive thinking strategies because readers justify answers when they supply supporting details.

Outline Frames

Many students have difficulty dealing with the structure and organization of expository text (Meyer, Brandt, & Bluth, 1980; Taylor, 1980). They may not recognize a main idea and realize that it is supported by details or examples. Consequently, recall after reading might consist solely of irrelevant or unconnected facts. Taylor (1982) found the hierarchical summary procedure helpful in directing middlegrade students' attention to the organization of ideas in content textbooks and in increasing the amount of information remembered after reading.

In the first step of the hierarchical summary procedure, with the aid of a teacher, students generate a skeleton outline for a segment of a textbook. Roman numerals and capital letters are used to designate major sections and subsections. Five or six lines are left between capital letters so students can write important supporting details as they read. After reading, the details are discussed and, with the teacher's help, a main idea and a few important supporting details are identified. Finally, students study the material and retell orally what they have learned.

A modification of the hierarchical summary procedure can be used as an assessment device. Students are presented with a skeleton outline that contains the major headings and subheadings from a reading selection and told to complete the outline while reading the passage. Words or phrases supplied indicate clearly whether the student can recognize supporting details. Variations of this procedure call for skeleton outlines in which details are given but subheadings are not provided. The latter variation is not suggested for elementary school children; however, it has been helpful in diagnosing the reading difficulties of high school students.

The hierarchical summary procedure was developed to be an instructional method. Like all good teaching strategies, it can become an assessment tool when the students' learning behaviors are carefully observed. When this tool is used over a period of time, teachers may get a more accurate assessment of students' abilities than they would secure from a single reading test. A seventh grade girl named Cara exemplifies the necessity for going beyond the test. Although test results indicated that she could read at the eighth grade level, Cara was receiving below average grades. When presented with a skeleton outline, she completed it satisfactorily. However, in future sessions, when Cara was asked to develop an outline, she was not able to do it. This inability to recognize and organize important information prevented her from taking relevant notes and summarizing reading selections. Thus, her achievement in content subjects was unsatisfactory.

The completion of outlines is an activity suitable for single session testing as well as ongoing diagnostic teaching. Over a period of time, teachers get an accurate assessment of students' abilities to recognize main ideas and supporting details, to scan and skim materials in order to locate specific information, and to sequence facts and events.

Summary

This chapter emphasizes the importance of reaching beyond traditional test scores for diagnostic information. Since human beings tend to be unpredictable, informal procedures that can be used in ongoing diagnostic teaching often yield more accurate information about a student's reading ability than tests used in a single testing session. In addition to yielding evaluative advice, the strategies described in this chapter can help students formulate a structure for assimilating and retaining the important information they derive from print.

References

Adams, M.J., and Collins, A. A schema-theoretic view of reading. In H. Singer and R.B. Ruddell (Eds.), *Theoretical models and processes of reading.* Newark, DE: International Reading Association, 1985.
Baron, R.A., Byrne, D., and Kantowitz, B.H. *Psychology: Understanding behavior.* Philadelphia: W.B. Saunders, 1977.

Edmiaston, R.K. Oral language and reading: How are they related for third graders? *Remedial and Special Education*, 1985, *5*, 33-37.

Fowler, G.L. Developing comprehension skills in primary students through the use of story frames. *The Reading Teacher*, 1982, *36*, 176-179.

Frose, V., and Kurushima, S. The effects of sentence expansion practice on the reading comprehension and writing ability of third graders. In M.L. Kamil and A.J. Moe (Eds.), *Reading research: Studies and applications*, twenty-eighth yearbook of the National Reading Conference. Rochester, NY: National Reading Conference, 1979.

Gambrell, L., Pfeiffer, W., and Wilson, R. The effects of retelling upon reading comprehension and recall of text information. *Journal of Educational Research*, 1985, *78*, 216-220.

Glazer, S.M., and Searfoss, L.W. *Reading diagnosis and instruction: A C-A-L-M approach*. Englewood Cliffs, NJ: Prentice-Hall, 1988.

Individualized language arts. Weehawken, NJ: Weehawken High School, 1974.

Irwin, P.A., and Mitchell, J. A procedure for assessing the richness of retellings. *Journal of Reading*, 1983, *26*, 391-396.

Johnston, P., and Pearson, P.D. *Prior knowledge, connectivity, and the assessment of reading comprehension*. Technical Report No. 245. Champaign, IL: University of Illinois, Center for the Study of Reading, 1982.

Laine, J.E. A language analysis of successful and nonsuccessful readers: Comparing linguistic ability in Black, Chicano, and Anglo boys. *Journal of Black Studies*, 1978, *8*, 439-451.

Lefevre, C. *Linguistics, English, and the language arts*. Boston: Allyn & Bacon, 1970.

Meyer, B.J.F., Brandt, D.M., and Bluth, G.J. Use of top level structure in text: Key for reading comprehension of ninth grade students. *Reading Research Quarterly*, 1980, *16*, 72-103.

Neville, D., and Searls, E. The effect of sentence combining and kernel identification training on the syntactic component of reading comprehension. *Research in the Teaching of English*, 1985, *19*, 37-61.

Nichols, J. Using paragraph frames to help remedial high school students with written assignment comprehension. *New Y*, 1980, *24*, 228-231.

Rumelhart, D.E. Understanding understanding. In J. Flood (Ed.), *Understanding reading comprehension*. Newark, DE: International Reading Association, 1984.

Stein, N., and Glenn, C. An analysis of story comprehension in elementary school children. In R.A. Freedle (Ed.), *New directions in discourse processes*. Norwood, NJ: Ablex, 1979.

Strong, W. Sentence-combining: Back to the basics and beyond. *English Journal*, 1976, *65*, 60-64.

Taylor, B.M. A summarizing strategy to improve middle grade students' reading and writing skills. *The Reading Teacher*, 1982, *36*, 202-205.

Taylor, B.M. Children's memory for expository text after reading. *Reading Research Quarterly*, 1980, *15*, 399-411.

Carol S. Brown
Susan L. Lytle

7

Merging Assessment and Instruction: Protocols in the Classroom

Assessment and instruction in reading typically occur as separate activities in school. The two often are assumed to have different goals and audiences, to require distinct methods, and to use different materials. The task of assessing may fall to specialists who work outside classrooms, so teachers have difficulty using the findings to make instructional decisions. In many cases, assessing and teaching are the responsibility of different staff members within a school system, so the reading specialist or school psychologist may be responsible for assessment while the classroom teacher is in charge of instruction. Yet much can be achieved from integrating these two activities: Teachers can gather data systematically while teaching and students can self-assess actively while learning. Teachers can respond immediately to the data gathered while students become informed partners in their learning.

This chapter argues for the importance of integrating assessment and instruction in reading and for using think aloud protocols in teaching. Protocols focus teachers' and students' attention on the processes of learning, thus providing information about students' metacognitive behaviors before, during, and after reading. They can be used as a structure for whole class or small group activities as well as a framework for thinking or writing about what has been read.

Why Integrate Assessment?

Although school structures typically maintain distinctions between assessment and instruction in reading, there are theoretical

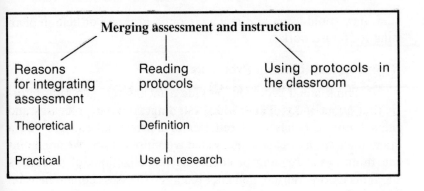

Merging assessment and instruction

Reasons for integrating assessment

Theoretical

Practical

Reading protocols

Definition

Use in research

Using protocols in the classroom

and practical reasons for not doing so. Current theories of reading describe the processes of gaining meaning from print as a constructive activity in which the reader gradually builds an understanding of the text (Collins, Brown, & Larkin, 1980; Rummelhart, 1977; Spiro, 1980). This process is dynamic, with readers continuing to formulate meaning throughout the entire task and often revising their interpretations through rereading, rethinking, or writing about what has been read. Although teachers' questions after reading may be viewed as assessment within instruction, one could argue that this focus on products gives teachers and students little insight into how the learners arrived at the answers.

A second theoretical perspective supporting the integration of assessment and instruction emphasizes the contextual nature of reading. We know from sociolinguistic research that home, school, and community contexts demand a variety of functions and uses for reading, and thus a diverse set of tasks and strategies (e.g., Bloome & Green, 1984). In school, combining assessment with instruction makes it more likely that the information gained from the assessment will be ecologically valid. Instead of testing reading, protocols can be used to assess readers' processes in context, within naturally occurring reading tasks.

From a practical perspective, separating assessment from instruction creates problems for classroom teachers who lack the time to do frequent, in depth assessments of individual students. Although group assessments of prior knowledge and progress are essential for planning lessons, information often is not obtained on readers' processes of comprehension. If teachers had the information, they could use it to direct a lesson in progress or help in planning for future work.

Think Aloud Reading Protocols

Think aloud protocols provide a means for gathering information about individual readers' ongoing thinking processes and metacognitive behavior. Used flexibly, protocols can provide a framework for assessment integrated with instruction. We are defining think aloud reading protocols as verbalizations of a reader's thoughts before, during, and after reading. To assess comprehension in process, readers are asked to read a portion of text and then to voice their thoughts. Directions asking readers to report such thoughts as "news bulletins or play by play accounts of where you are intellectually as you figure out what the reading is about" (Lytle, 1982, p. 113) may be used to help readers understand what they might talk about.

Origins of the use of various think aloud procedures to study reading can be traced back to Huey's 1908 use of retrospection and introspection to study college students' understanding of vocabulary words. Since then there has been sporadic use of verbal report procedures in research on reading processes, with more attention to this method in the past decade. Sparked by current interest in the processes of reading, this increased use of verbal reports can be seen by the small but growing number of researchers who have used think aloud protocols in studying readers' thinking behavior (see, for example, Bereiter & Bird, 1985; Collins, Brown, & Larkin, 1980; Lytle, 1982; Olshavsky, 1975, 1977).

Protocols have been used to study a variety of topics including readers' use of genre conventions (Olson, Mack, & Duffy, 1981), the effects of readers' purposes for reading on their understanding (Waern, 1979), contextual effects on recall (Christopherson, Shultz, & Waern, 1981), second language learners' strategies (Hosenfeld, 1979), second language learners' reading of specialized discourse (Cohen et al., 1979), individual differences in comprehension style (Lytle, 1982), readers' strategies for understanding problematic expository text (Scardamalia & Bereiter, 1984), and readers' processing of poetry (Kintgen, 1985).

Think aloud protocols and protocol like activities also have been used in teaching procedures developed to affect students' ongoing thinking while reading. These include Bird's (1980) direct teaching approach, Palincsar and Brown's (1984) reciprocal teaching, and C. Brown's (1986) interactive protocol procedure. As part of her approach, Bird had entire classes of seventh graders make whispered protocols while she walked around listening. She also modeled specific responses to text and used individual protocols as a measure of change in reading-thinking processes. Palincsar and Brown and C. Brown combined protocols with assessment in more open ended procedures that focused on readers' moment to moment responses to text. Basing their process on Manzo's ReQuest procedure, Palincsar, and Brown used a protocol like activity with individuals, small groups, and naturally occurring classroom groups. They preselected four comprehension monitoring/fostering activities to teach in a turn taking procedure emphasizing teacher modeling and corrective feedback. C. Brown used interrupted protocols to focus college students' attention on their metacognitive processes and to foster expansion of their characteristic responses to text. Reading protocols also have been used by investigators as part of assessment procedures. Myers and Lytle (1986) suggest the use of protocols as part of what they call Process Assessment, a model for assessing children with learning problems. The model evaluates the processes of learning by focusing on the task, the child, and the environment.

Several of these studies provide a framework for analyzing protocol data and a method for using protocols in classroom instruction. Lytle (1986) developed an analytic coding system called Types of Moves to describe the responses of secondary age readers to difficult texts. Types of Moves contains six major categories and twenty-one subcategories. Lytle used the term *move* to describe the "verbal response of readers to sentences in the text" (p. 17) or what readers do as they make their way through the text. The six major categories included Monitoring of Doubts, Signaling Understanding, Analyzing Text Features, Elaboration of the Text, Judgment of the Text, and Reasoning. Lytle describes each category as representing a different type of statement or question readers ask themselves and answer as they read. She illustrates this relationship as follows

(p. 127):

Monitoring.	I don't understand. This doesn't make sense.
Signaling.	What do I know?
Analyzing.	How does this text work?
Elaborating.	What does this make me think of?
Judging.	How good is this?
Reasoning.	How can I figure this out? What might x mean?

She also uses the term *strategy* to refer to "goal directed segments or sequences" of moves (1982, p. 17). Strategies are patterns of moves in response to doubt, i.e., the moves readers make after noticing they don't understand what they have read. In Lytle's study her subjects responded to doubt by using their own preferred sequences of moves, or strategies. In Lytle's framework (p. 18), reading style consists of "the overall pattern of an individual's moves and strategies within and across texts." The notion of style can be used to describe readers' propensities to respond to text. In Lytle's study, readers' styles were found to be consistent across three nonfiction texts that differed in length, subject matter, and other features. She concluded that a reader's pattern of moves and strategies provides a lens for understanding intra as well as inter individual differences, as long as these differences are carefully related to the specific task and context.

C. Brown (1986) used interrupted protocols in an instructional program designed to increase readers' metacongitive awareness. The Interactive Protocol Procedure (IPP) interjects suggestions to the student about further ways to respond to the text while the student is making a think aloud protocol. These suggestions are based on Lytle's Types of Moves and focus on students' use of the six major categories of moves, their strategies, and thus their reading style. In the IPP, the tutor moves gradually from general to specific suggestions through a series of questions that assist the reader in thinking about the text. They begin with nondirective responses displaying interest and attention and only gradually become more intrusive in the student's thinking by suggesting and finally, where needed, modeling moves and strategies. Results of use of the IPP with college students in tutorial settings showed changes in their use of moves and strategies.

Think Aloud Protocols in the Classroom

Work by Lytle (1982) and C. Brown (1986) suggests that think aloud protocols and the concepts of move, strategy, and style can be integrated into instructional programs that may affect individual reader's thinking processes while reading. Here we are recommending classroom use of protocols in a variety of ways for a range of purposes, all focusing on readers' processes. The goal is to increase both students' metacognitive awareness and their repertoire of possible responses to text. For example, a teacher working with a small group of students could guide them in making a group protocol. One purpose of a group working together is to demonstrate to the students how much thinking readers should do in the process of understanding text and making a protocol. Students may be willing to expose their thinking in a small group where they feel comfortable. The teacher could begin by reading a short problematic text to the students one sentence at a time. As the students respond orally the teacher could jot their ideas on the board, gradually constructing a protocol of the group's responses to the text. Examples of this type of text follow.

a.
1. He plunked down $5 at the window.
2. She tried to give him $2.50, but he refused to take it.
3. When they got inside, she bought him a large bag of popcorn (Collins, Brown, & Larkin, 1980, p. 387).

b.
1. He stared at the bright ring with fear.
2. As he moved closer to the ring, people began to shout.
3. In nine rounds he might be the champ.

When the students are finished talking, they might read their comments and discuss their various responses to the text. If teachers want a specific type of response (i.e., hypothesis or prediction) included in this discussion, they could model it while the group is making the protocol. Students will probably notice comments pertaining to things they remember or experiences they have had, things they may notice about the way the text is written, things they do not understand, or questions about meaning.

The next step is to put a short text on an overhead projector. Students can take turns, responding to chunks of texts as they are uncovered. In case teachers want to use students' comments later, they could jot them on the board, on paper, or on a chart or tape record the group. An alternative method of presenting the text would be to have students move an index card down the pages of their books, exposing some prescribed portion of the text and then discussing it. Protocols made in small groups provide assessment information that can be immediately integrated into the lesson. For example, when students verbalize a lack of understanding in the midst of reading, classmates or teachers can share their own thinking about the passage, thus providing examples of additional responses to the text that might help the student resolve the problem.

Another example of classroom use of protocols to integrate assessment and instruction could be as a guide for whole class discussion of a particularly difficult section of a chapter. During a typical discussion, teachers ask questions and students answer. Protocols focus on the process of constructing answers. Students can make protocols from the title, subtitle, or first sentence and at several points during and immediately after reading. Teachers can suggest that students write responses while reading. Jottings of thoughts during reading can serve readily as written protocols to be shared later. It may be particularly beneficial to focus on students' lack of understanding and what they did next. Students who shared the same confusion may discover they used different thinking. Some students may have thought about related experiences they had, while others searched for evidence in the text to support their hypotheses about the meaning. Sharing these differences highlights strategy use and can affect students' reading styles.

A final example of protocols in the classroom is their use in teaching writing. A protocol made by a classmate can guide a student's revising. Writing conference partners can sit together and take

turns making think aloud protocols from one another's composi-
tions, essay questions, letters, lab reports, or stories. The metaphor
"movies of the mind" may give the partners insight into what they
can discuss in these protocols. They are to let their partners hear
how they are making sense of the text. Students get immediate feedback on their writing as they listen to the tentative efforts of a reader
trying to understand what they have written. These protocol like
conferences can help students revise for a specific audience, with
specific comprehension problems in mind. New protocols made by
the same partners from the revised drafts can examine the success of
their efforts.

One important effect the use of protocols has on students'
reading at all levels is to slow down the comprehending process.
This additional time helps students think about the ideas in the text
and about the thinking processes readers use in understanding them.
Such attention to reading processes stimulates students to broaden
their responses to text, to develop a repertoire of ways to think in
response to what they read. We are not suggesting teaching methods
of thinking out of the context of actual reading events; we are advo-
cating an emphasis on having students verbalize their spontaneous
responses to text before, during, and after reading. Moves and strategies are not subskills of reading and should not be drilled or taught
as discrete elements. In contrast to a subskills approach, we are suggesting a variety of group interactions that may help individual students orchestrate their own thinking processes when reading
independently. Protocols offer a means of eliciting and reflecting on
these processes.

Summary

Think aloud protocols offer potential for integrating assessment and instruction in reading. Because protocols reveal some of
the thinking used in comprehending text, they focus attention on students' metacognitive processes in reading. This attention provides a
means of sharing and reflecting on individual reader's thinking processes and of guiding group work in responding to text. In addition, it
places assessment in a context where classroom teachers can imme-

diately use findings to make instructional decisions and students can become more informed partners in the learning process.

References

Bereiter, C., and Bird, M. Use of thinking aloud in identification and teaching of reading comprehension strategies. *Cognition and Instruction*, 1985, *2* (2), 131-156.

Bird, M. *Reading comprehension strategies: A direct teaching approach,* doctoral dissertation, University of Toronto, 1980. *Dissertation Abstracts International*, 1980, *41* (6) 2506-A.

Bloome, D., and Green, J. Directions in the sociolinguistic study of reading. In P.D. Pearson (Ed.), *Handbook of reading research.* New York: Longman, 1984, 395-421.

Brown, C. *A tutorial procedure for enhancing the reading comprehension of college students,* doctoral dissertation, University of Pennsylvania, 1986. *Dissertation Abstracts International, 47* (10), 3719-A.

Christopherson, S., Schultz, C., and Waern, Y. The effects of two contextual conditions on recall of a reading passage and on thought processes in reading. *Journal of Reading,* 1981, *24* (7), 573-578.

Cohen, A., Glasman, H., Rosenbaum-Cohen, P., Ferrera, J., and Fine, J. Reading English for specialized purposes: Discourse analysis and the use of student informants. *TESOL Quarterly,* 1979, *13* (4), 551-564.

Collins, A., Brown, J., and Larkin, K. Inference in text understanding. In R. Spiro, B. Bruce, and W. Brewer (Eds.). *Theoretical issues in reading comprehension.* Hillsdale, NJ: Erlbaum, 1980, 385-407.

Hosenfeld, C. Cindy: A learner in today's foreign language classroom. In W. Borne (Ed.), *The foreign language learner in today's classroom environment.* Montpelier, VT: Northeast Conference on the Teaching of Foreign Languages, 1979, 53-75.

Huey, E. *The psychology and pedagogy of reading.* New York: Macmillan, 1908.

Kintgen, E. Studying the perception of poetry. In C. Cooper (Ed.), *Researching response to literature.* Norwood, NJ: Ablex, 1985, 128-150.

Lytle, S.L. *Exploring comprehension style: A study of twelfth grade readers' transactions with text,* doctoral dissertation, University of Pennsylvania, 1982. *Dissertation Abstracts International, 43* (7), 2295-A.

Manzo, A.V. Improving reading comprehension through reciprocal questioning. *Dissertation Abstracts International,* 1968, *30,* 5344-A.

Myers, J., and Lytle, S. Assessment of the learning process. *Exceptional Children,* 1986, *53* (2), 138-144.

Olshavsky, J. An exploratory analysis of the reading process. *Dissertation Abstracts International,* 1975, *36* (9), 5975-A.

Olshavsky, J. Reading as problem solving: An investigation of strategies. *Reading Research Quarterly,* 1977, *12* (4), 654-674.

Olson, G., Mack, R., and Duffy, S. Cognitive aspects of genre. *Poetics,* 1981, *10,* 283-315.

Palincsar, A.S., and Brown, A.L. Reciprocal teaching of comprehension fostering and comprehension monitoring activities. *Cognition and Instruction,* 1984, *1* (2), 117-175.

Rummelhart, D. Toward an interactive model of reading. In S. Doric (Ed.), *Attention and performance VI.* London: Academic Press, 1977.

Scardamalia, M., and Bereiter, C. Development of strategies in text processing. In H. Mandl, N. Stein, and T. Trebasso (Eds.), *Learning and comprehension of text.* Hillsdale, NJ: Erlbaum, 1984.

Spiro, R. Constructive processes in prose comprehension and recall. In R. Spiro, B. Bruce, and W. Brewer (Eds.), *Theoretical issues in reading comprehension.* Hillsdale, NJ: Erlbaum, 1980.

Waern, Y. *Thinking aloud during reading: A descriptive model and its application,* No. 546. Stockholm, Sweden: Report from the Department of Psychology, The University of Stockholm, 1979.

Organizing and Retaining Information by Thinking Like an Author

T his chapter introduces recent thinking about the role of an author's structure in middle and secondary students' comprehension. It describes a process for observing, assessing, and improving students' understanding of text structure.

The first part of the chapter discusses research identifying various forms of text structure and their impact on student comprehension and recall; the next part offers a rationale for observation of students' intuitive grasp of text structure using a think aloud protocol; and the last part provides specific strategies to enhance students' understanding of text structure.

Research on Text Structure

Most people who are successful in high school and college have a well developed yet unconscious sense of how authors structure ideas in both narrative and expository texts. This tacit schema for text structure helps us predict oncoming information in a text and acts as a framework for retrieval of text information. Even if you don't know much about the specific elements of a story grammar, you can use your experiences reading narratives to reconstruct a decomposed story. The following story consists of randomly ordered passages that need to be reordered into a normal story sequence. See if you can reorganize this story into a well formed structure easier to comprehend. Place a number next to each section of the story to indicate its normal position (i.e., 1, first section; 2, second section).

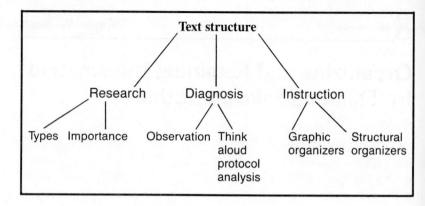

The Accomplice

___ Phyllis hesitated, then raised her hand to tell Mrs. Hampton what she saw. Unfortunately, eight other hands also were raised in response to the question about the U.S. Constitution.

"Jim?" Mrs Hampton ignored Phyllis as usual, and Jim rambled on about various amendments. Meanwhile, the car thief was making his getaway in Mrs. Hampton's new red Supra.

___ A highly skilled car thief stalked the faculty parking lot just after school started.

___ Phyllis held her arm higher, cradling it in her other hand, but Mrs. Hampton continued to ignore her. Finally, she lowered her hand and stared at the vacant parking spot where Mrs. Hampton's car was only moments ago. She thought to herself that Mrs. Hampton would get a real surprise that afternoon and Phyllis would be there to watch.

___ Phyllis saw him through the window just as he jimmied the lock on Mrs. Hampton's new Toyota Supra. The man opened the door and stepped inside.

If you sequenced this scrambled story in the following order you have an intuitive sense of story structure.

1. A highly skilled car thief.
2. Phyllis saw him through the window. . . .
3. Phyllis hesitated, then raised her hand. . . .
4. Phyllis held her arm higher. . . .

This underlying sense of an author's structure also applies to expository text. In the section that follows, both forms of text will be described in detail with comments about current research findings.

If we could place a group of people in a waiting room similar to a dentist's outer office and watch them through a two way mirror as they selected reading material from a nearby coffee table, what might we observe? Chances are, given a choice between *People* magazine, *Business Weekly, Science,* and *National Geographic,* the majority would battle over *People.* Why? Because *People* naturally captures human interest but also because it most closely resembles the narrative form of text structure—a form that has its roots in the ancient oral tradition of story telling. Most of us prefer stories over exposition because stories are captivating and memorable (Graesser, 1981). During the past ten years a number of cognitive scientists and linguists have been exploring how readers represent stories in memory and what role story structure plays in this process.

Narrative structures typically contain the following major categories: setting, initiating event, internal response, attempts, consequence, and reaction. Applying these categories to "The Accomplice," you can see that the setting is in Mrs. Hampton's classroom where Phyllis, our protagonist, is seen gazing out the window. Readers expect the setting to be the first category they encounter in a well formed story. Next, we see Phyllis spot the car thief, thus supplying our story with an initiating event to get it moving. Phyllis' response to this event initially is one of concern for Mrs. Hampton's car and she raises her hand to warn Mrs. Hampton. Her attempt to act is thwarted when Mrs. Hampton ignores Phyllis. As a result, Phyllis reacts by lowering her hand as the teacher's car is stolen from the parking lot. Phyllis gets her own form of revenge for being ignored by Mrs. Hampton and, in a sense, becomes an "accomplice" in the theft of the car.

We know that recall of story information is better for students who are able to use an author's structure as a retrieval cue. Poorer readers seem to benefit most from direct instruction in story structure (McGee & Richgels, 1986; Pearson & Camperell, 1985). Although most students have a good internal sense of story structure by third grade, students who are experiencing real difficulty in reading comprehension may benefit from more attention in this area. The question is, how can a teacher determine in a valid and reliable way if a student has a good grasp of story structure? That question and its application to expository text structure will be discussed later.

Although middle and secondary students may have excellent senses of story structure, this is rarely true as they read increasingly complex expository texts in social science and science (McGee & Richgels, 1986). Unlike the friendly narrative pattern that has its roots in an oral tradition, expository text uses multiple structures often interleaved within a single text and sometimes highly specific to certain content areas (e.g., structure function patterns in biology). The most common text patterns students encounter include the following described by Readence, Bean, and Baldwin (1985):*

1. *Cause/Effect.* This pattern links reasons with results. It is characterized by an interaction between at least two ideas or events, one taking an action and another resulting from that action. Social studies texts often use this pattern.

Example. The heavy snowfall prevented the climbers from going to the top of the mountain.

2. *Comparison/Contrast.* This pattern discusses and illustrates apparent likenesses and differences between two or more things.

Example. Surfing and snow skiing share similar maneuvers but in surfing you have to paddle out to the waves and in skiing a lift takes you up the mountain.

3. *Time Order.* This pattern shows a sequential relationship between ideas or events considered in the presence of the passage of time.

Example. During the fall semester, John did the research for his dissertation. In the spring he completed writing his dissertation and was interviewed for a position in Australia that will begin this summer.

4. *Simple Listing.* This pattern is characterized by a listing of items or ideas. The order of the items is not significant.

Example. Margaret got everything she needed to paint the fence — a dropcloth, brushes, thinner, paint, and her hat.

5. *Problem/Solution.* Similar to the cause/effect pattern, this pattern is exemplified by an interaction between at least two factors, one citing a problem and another providing a potential answer to that problem.

Example. Failing to remember things is a problem that plagues most of us. Fortunately, a simple solution involves making a list of items that would otherwise slip from our memories.

6. *Argument.* This pattern unveils pro and con arguments concerning a topic, ultimately supporting some favored view.

Example. Skateboards should be banned on college campuses. While they provide low cost transportation for students between classes, they are responsible for an increasing number of accidents.

*From *Reading in the Content Areas* by Readence-Bean-Baldwin. Copyright © 1985 by Kendall/Hunt Publishing Company. Used with permission.

These six expository text structures represent macrostructures writers and readers can use to portray ideas in a memorable fashion. In recent reviews synthesizing over ten years of research into the effects of text structure on students' comprehension, the overwhelming conclusion is that familiarity with these structures enhances comprehension (McGee & Richgels, 1986; Richgels et al., 1987). Furthermore, direct instruction in expository patterns can increase comprehension (Pearson & Camperell, 1985). Research conducted by Meyer and reviewed by Meyer and Rice (1984) suggests that certain patterns seem to be more memorable than others. For example, a text that argues a point with pro and con arguments may be easier to remember than a text that simply provides information about a topic. In fact, fluent readers often argue with text that simply presents information in a dull, linear list in order to maintain attention and increase memory for the information being discussed (Alvermann, 1982). In addition to these macrostructure patterns, each has signal words that occur at the microstructure level, although authors frequently omit any explicit signals to a text's macrostructure.

Cause/effect patterns often contain signal words like *because, since, therefore, consequently,* and *as a result.*

Comparison/contrast patterns use signal words like *however, but, as well as, on the other hand,* and *similarly.*

Time order patterns may use *not long after, now, after,* and *before.*

Simple listing typically uses words like *to begin with, first, second, next,* and *finally.*

Research by Meyer, Brandt, and Bluth (1980) found that ninth grade students could be taught to use highlighted signal words to identify a text's structure and increase their recall of important information. But again, how does a teacher determine if students have an internal sense of expository text patterns? The section that follows describes a procedure for observing and judging students' understanding of narrative and expository text structures.

Observation of Text Structure Understanding

The idea of observing students as they read and discuss ideas in a text to determine the degree to which they are able to think like a writer may not seem very revolutionary. However, since the early 1900s assessment in reading has been mired in a medical model with the goal of assessment being a search for deficits in the reader and some related internal cause (Lipson & Wixson, 1986). Rose (1985) traced a similar remedial view of assessment in writing that grew out of the 1900s desire for objective, teacher proof measures. Applied to writing, this form of assessment meant a search for grammatical errors rather than an attempt to understand the process a fledgling writer uses to explore ideas. In reading assessment, this desire for efficient scientific management of the schools led to objective tests consisting of passage dependent literal questions covering short passages (Moore, 1986).

In contrast to end product, error centered measures, naturalistic assessment requires observation of students' reading in multiple settings (Lipson & Wixson, 1986, Moore, 1986; Glazer & Searfoss, this volume). The first setting to use as a point of observation is the normal day to day classroom. Be on the lookout for signals that students are using an author's text structure to their advantage. What signals should you look for? Following are some signals of text structure awareness:

1. When students are retelling a story or discussing an expository selection, do they seem to use the author's organizational structure as their retelling or comments unfold?

2. When students are writing summaries or essays based on text reading, are there indications they are using text structure knowledge as a framework for developing their writing?

3. As you observe students taking notes, outlining, mapping or graphically depicting text ideas, is there a pattern that shows they are using text structure cues to learn the concepts in a text?

Naturally, this form of observation requires you to have a clear sense of the text structure patterns that occur in your classroom. Based on these informal observations during the normal flow of instruction, you may well identify some students who appear to have only a partial or minimal understanding of text structure cues and their use in comprehension and writing. If so, you can then move to a more detailed observation of an individual student's text structure understanding in a reading conference. This more detailed observation involves the use of a talk aloud protocol and decomposed text like "The Accomplice" story you reconstructed at the beginning of this chapter. Brown and Lytle's chapter in this book provides a detailed description of how to use think aloud protocol analysis. The process of diagnosing students' text structure understanding will be illustrated for expository and narrative text after a brief description of think aloud protocol analysis.

Think Aloud Protocol Analysis

Think aloud protocols have been used by reading researchers to gain a window on the reading process of elementary and secondary students (e.g., Olshavsky, 1977). Although there is some variation in the process of conducting a think aloud session, depending on the purposes desired, the following guidelines are appropriate for a session focusing on the assessment of a student's understanding of text structure.

The actual text material you use for a think aloud session should be the normal text students are required to read in your class. Tell students they will be reading a story or text that is mixed-up. Ask students to read each section of the text you have cut up at paragraph boundaries and shuffled. It is helpful to have each section color coded. For example, you might code the beginning dark blue, the middle yellow, and so on. That way, it will be relatively easy to relate students' think aloud commentaries with various sections of the story. To prepare the material for a session, simply shuffle the text sections into random order as you would a deck of cards. It is also a good idea to tape record the session for later analysis.

You need to write a script to introduce a student to a think aloud session so the process will go smoothly. The following script is adapted from Lytle (1982).

Think Aloud Script for Assessing Text Structure Understanding

I am going to give you a story (or text) to read and put together the way you, as an author, would write it. The story (or text) is divided into paragraph sections that are mixed up. Call each section by the colored dot on it.

Read each section to yourself silently. Tell me the color before you begin reading. Then read the section and tell me what you are doing and thinking about as you try to see where this section fits in the whole story. I will just listen and not nod or anything; in fact, this is more like talking to yourself—"thinking aloud." I am interested in what you say to yourself as you read, what you are thinking about as you go along.

After you have read the first color coded section and told everything you are thinking, go on to the next section mentioning its color. In a way, you are then telling what you are thinking about two sections of the story (or text), and then three, and so on—kind of news bulletins or play by play accounts of where you are in your thoughts as you try to figure out how to put the story together so it makes sense.

If you get stuck or have trouble understanding, I would like to hear about that too and try to figure out a solution to what's puzzling you.

After you have read and talked about each section, and put the story together the way you as an author think it should go, I'd like to have you reflect for a while and then tell me your own sense of what the story was about. You can look back at the story if you like, but try to recall the basic ideas in your own words.

While you are doing this, I will say nothing. I will have a small notebook open because I may want to write a few notes to myself—things that occur to me as you talk about the story. I know I will have the tape to listen to but I have found that I sometimes can't remember ideas unless I write them.

In order to illustrate the use of think aloud protocols in observing a student's sense of text structure, a session showing a fluent college age reader reconstructing the campfire horror story, "Cold and Clammy" (Christen, Searfoss, & Bean, 1984), will be discussed. Lytle (1982) has developed a system for analyzing observations of students' think aloud protocols that will be used to consider the students' transcript. But first, here is the complete "Cold and Clammy" story in the correct sequence.

Cold and Clammy*

Sue and Eve were nursing students who occupied the same apartment. Sue was pretty, vivacious, and always had plenty of dates. She also greatly enjoyed playing practical jokes on other people. Eve was just the opposite, quiet, somewhat withdrawn, though also very intelligent.

The two had a minor argument one morning, and Sue decided to get even with Eve. Sue knew that Eve would be studying late at the library that evening, as usual. So she concocted a plan.

They were dissecting cadavers in her nursing class, and it would be easy for Sue to secretly remove an arm from class. First, she would attach the cold, clammy, dead arm to the light switch in the apartment. The switch was the kind with a chain you pull in order to turn on the light. That was the difficult part since the arm was so bulky and unwieldy and the switch so flimsy. Sue used a thin rope and fastened it to one end of the arm and hooked the other end to a nail in the ceiling next to the switch. If someone reached for the switch, they would grasp the arm instead!

Soon after 10:30, Eve could be heard fumbling at the door, struggling to get her key into the keyhole. She mumbled something about Sue's always forgetting to leave the porch light on for her, and then she entered the gloomy room. She took a few tentative steps and reached up to turn on the light. Nothing happened!

The neighbors later reported that there were no strange noises or screams from the house until after Sue had returned home and found Eve. When Sue did come home, she was laughing as she opened the door. Entering the dark room, she hoped that Eve had already returned and made the grisly discovery. She turned on the light and was surprised to find Eve standing in the middle of the room clutching the arm. Eve's hair turned white! She was in shock and was destined to never recover. Later, she was committed to an institution for the hopelessly insane and wasted her promising life.

Sue probably would never play a joke on anyone again.

*From *Improving Communication through Writing and Reading by* Christen-Searfoss-Bean. Copyright © 1984 by Kendall/Hunt Publishing Company. Used with permission.

Lytle's (1982) system for analyzing think aloud protocols contains six moves a reader is likely to make in attempting to comprehend a text. These moves are:
  1. *Monitoring.* I don't understand. This doesn't make sense. Manifested in statements or questions indicating the reader doubts his/her understanding (including conflicts).
  2. *Signaling.* What do I understand? Manifested in statements in which the reader signals his/

her current understanding of the text's meaning (agrees, paraphrases, summarizes).
3. *Analyzing.* How does this text work?
Manifested in statements in which the reader, viewing the text as an object, notices, describes, or comments on the features of text (e.g., words, sentences, text structure, style). Thus, for the purpose of observing a reader's sense of text structure, we would expect to see this move occur within the think aloud process.
4. *Elaborating.* What does this make me think of?
Manifested in statements describing the ways the reader is responding to or experiencing the text such as imagery, recalling prior knowledge, liking/disliking.
5. *Judging.* How good is this?
Manifested in statements indicating the reader is evaluating the text (ideas or text features).
6. *Reasoning.* How can I figure this out? What might X mean?
Manifested in statements or questions indicating the reader is trying to resolve doubts and interpret the text (e.g., hypothesis, prediction, question, use of evidence).

The student reconstructing this story is named Vicki. After listening to the script describing the task of thinking aloud while putting the story back together in the fashion of an author, Vicki received the following scrambled version of the story. Notice that each section of the story is color coded. The story parts are labeled in this version but they were not part of the version Vicki received.

Cold and Clammy

black (initiating event)

The two had a minor argument one morning, and Sue decided to get even with Eve. Sue knew that Eve would be studying late at the library that evening, as usual. So she concocted a plan.

Vicki: Okay. This is probably at the beginning of the story. There could be some other things that happened but something has been happening before this because she concocted a plan. So obviously she's been thinking she needs to get something done. So something happened before so Sue probably wanted to get in touch with Eve. To do something with her.

In this instance, Vicki is analyzing the content of this section in order to determine where it fits in the flow of the story. At this point she has only this one section so her conclusions about its role in the story are tentative but she appears to have a good grasp of the story structure.

red (resolution)

The neighbors later reported that there were no strange noises or screams from the house until after Sue had returned home and found Eve. When Sue did come home, she was laughing as she opened the door. Entering the dark room, she hoped that Eve had already returned and made the grisly discovery. She turned on the light and was surprised to find Eve standing in the middle of the room clutching the arm. Eve's hair turned white! She was in shock and was destined to never recover. Later, she was committed to an institution for the hopelessly insane and wasted her promising life.

Vicki: This happened after black because Sue has . . . because it says Sue returned home and found Eve, so, I guess. . . .Well, maybe not, it could be. Most likely it happened after that. Obviously while Eve was at the library Sue set up something at home for Eve to return and discover. This is near the end.

Vicki uses the previous section of the story as a benchmark for comparison with this new section. Her initial response shows some confusion about this section's place in the story, largely because she began talking aloud before completing her reading of the passage. Her initial response displays features that correspond to Lytle's "reasoning" move. Once Vicki completes reading the passage she analyzes the section's position in the story with more assurance.

Again, Vicki illustrates a fluent reader treating a text as an object of analysis.

> green (outcome of attempt to achieve
> a goal or solve a problem)

Soon after 10:30, Eve could be heard fumbling at the door, struggling to get her key into the keyhole. She mumbled something about Sue's always forgetting to leave the porch light on for her, and then she entered the gloomy room. She took a few tentative steps and reached up to turn on the light. Nothing happened!

Vicki: This is Eve returning home. So this occurred before Sue got home and found Eve and all that.

> blue (main character's attempt to achieve a
> goal or solve a problem)

They were dissecting cadavers in her nursing class, and it would be easy for Sue to secretly remove an arm from class. First, she would attach the cold, clammy, dead arm to the light switch in the apartment. The switch was the kind with a chain you pull in order to turn on the light. That was the difficult part since the arm was so bulky and unwieldy and the switch so flimsy. Sue used a thin rope and fastened it to one end of the arm and hooked the other end to a nail in the ceiling next to the switch. If someone reached for the switch, they would grasp the arm instead!

Vicki: Okay. This is when Sue is setting up the thing for Eve. So, that comes before green.

At this stage in the process, Vicki has enough of the text and enough prior knowledge about story structure to quickly decide where each piece fits. Notice that her comments are confined to analyzing story structure rather than content, which is consistent with the purpose of this particular think aloud task.

> brown and red (ending and moral)

Sue probably would never play a joke on anyone again.

Vicki: That has to be the ending.

Sue and Eve were nursing students who occupied the same apartment. Sue was pretty, vivacious, and always had plenty of dates. She also greatly enjoyed playing practical jokes on other people. Eve was just the opposite, quiet, somewhat withdrawn, though also very intelligent.

Vicki: This is the beginning that's introducing who they are.

When Vicki was asked to retell the story she demonstrated a strong sense of the story's macrostructure. At this point it would have been a good idea to have Vicki reread the entire story in its original, cohesive form to ensure good comprehension before reflecting and retelling the story. Because Vicki did not do this, her retelling shows some confusion of events which she resolves by looking back at the story.

Vicki: Sue and Eve were nursing students. Sue decided to play a trick on Eve. While Eve was at the library, Sue went and got a cadaver's arm from their nursing class and attached it to a hanging light cord. So that when Eve came home the light switch wouldn't work so she had to walk over and pull on the cord to turn on the light. So she grabbed the arm. . . . No, that's not right. She grabbed the arm and the shock killed her. No, it didn't kill her—she went to an institution for the hopelessly insane.

Overall, Vicki's reconstruction of the story and subsequent retelling display three of Lytle's "moves." Given the nature of the reconstruction task, she analyzes text features. During the retelling, Vicki monitors and signals any hitches in her understanding and comfortably resolves them. In essence, Vicki has a well developed sense of story structure to guide her comprehension. Is her sense of text structure as strong in expository material? The next section shows Vicki's think aloud protocol for a brief problem solution passage concerning earthquakes (Christen, Searfoss, & Bean, 1984).

Earthquakes*

Earthquakes, in themselves, are not a significant hazard. The documented cases of a fault opening up and encompassing people and then burying them can, perhaps, be counted on one's fingers. Landslides can, and do, take a significant toll of lives, but in most cases these hazards are relatively self-evident before the earthquake and do not need an earthquake to trigger them. The major life hazard in the usual earthquake is from the collapse of man made structures such as buildings and dams. This is certainly true for all of California as well as San Francisco.

The solution to seismic hazards is to design and construct buildings in such a manner that they will remain safe during and after an earthquake, with damage limited to acceptable economic and functional levels. Ideally, then, an earthquake would become an exciting experience, but not a hazardous adventure.

However, tearing down all existing construction and replacing it with earthquake resistant construction has overwhelming limitations. Financial and material resources simply do not exist, technologies are inadequate for some cases, and only over time can these hazardous buildings be replaced.

At the local government level, the city of San Francisco is emulating the long established Los Angeles policy of removing or bracing all hazardous nonreinforced brick parapets and appendages. Worldwide earthquake experience clearly shows that these hazards are serious even in moderate shocks.

Vicki received this passage scrambled in the following fashion. She was given the whole passage rather than a section at a time because the passage is much less structured than a narrative.

yellow (limitations of the solution)

However, tearing down all existing construction and replacing it with earthquake resistant construction has overwhelming limitations. Financial and material resources simply do not exist, technologies are inadequate for some cases, and only over time can these hazardous buildings be replaced.

orange (problem)

Earthquakes, in themselves, are not a significant hazard. The documented cases of a fault opening up and encompassing people and then burying them can, perhaps, be counted on one's fingers. Landslides can, and do, take a significant toll of lives, but in most cases these hazards are relatively self-evident before the earthquake and do not need an earthquake to trigger them. The major life hazard in the usual earthquake is from the collapse of man made structures such as buildings and dams. This is certainly true for all of California as well as San Francisco.

brown (examples)

At the local government level, the city of San Francisco is emulating the long established Los Angeles policy of removing or bracing all hazardous nonreinforced brick parapets and appendages. Worldwide earthquake experience clearly shows that these hazards are serious even in moderate shocks.

blue (solution)

The solution to seismic hazards is to design and construct buildings in such a manner that they will remain safe during and after an earthquake, with damage limited to acceptable economic and functional levels. Ideally, then, an earthquake would become an exciting experience, but not a hazardous adventure.

The range of Vicki's comments as she assembled this expository passage were greater than in the narrative example. She displays a clear sense of structural cues, ultimately reconstructing the passage in a defensible fashion, albeit different from the author's. The following comments from her think aloud transcript reveal the process she went through in thinking like an author.

Vicki: This one is hard. Okay. The first one I'm going with is orange (the problem) because it talks about earthquakes. We'll see.

At this point, a fair amount of think time passes as she considers the other three sections of the passage.

Vicki: The solution. That one has to go last or toward the end. The brown one could be last too. However, yellow could go after brown. All right, let's see how this goes. Orange, blue, brown, and yellow. Help! I don't know how this goes together. I don't think this is a very good passage. Orange (the problem), brown (examples), yellow (limitations of the solution), and blue (solution).

Examining Vicki's final choice as an author shows a passage that, if anything, uses cohesive ties and transitions more effectively than the original passage. For example, the first paragraph ending with the reference to San Francisco leads logically into the example of how San Francisco is coping with the earthquake problem. Similarly, the next paragraph poses limitations of Los Angeles' expensive solution to the earthquake problem. Finally, the solution posed in the last paragraph seems to logically fit at the end, as Vicki suggests. The point is, a student may reconstruct an expository passage in a cohesive, sensible fashion that departs from the author's original structure. If this student's think aloud transcript shows evidence of sensitivity to text structure cues, comprehension of the passage is likely to be excellent. Indeed, Vicki's retelling of the earthquake passage indicated she had a clear grasp of its meaning.

Based on the two think aloud transcripts, Vicki does not appear to be a candidate for direct instruction in text structure cues. She already has a tacit understanding of signal words in texts and dominant patterns authors use to portray ideas. Not all students develop this awareness of text structure without teacher guidance, especially in the middle grades, junior high, and high school. The following example shows Brian, a sixth grader, attempting to reconstruct an expository passage about "Animal Hiding Places" (adapted from McCauley, 1986). The passage follows a problem solution structure and Brian does not seem to use this structure and some of the key words in the passage as he goes about thinking aloud and assembling the scrambled paragraphs. The original text is presented first, then Brian's think aloud.

Animal Hiding Places

Most animals face the problem of finding a good place to hide from their predators. Some animals are lucky enough to have a built-in disguise that helps them hide. (yellow)

A turtle tucks itself tightly inside its hard shell. It looks like a rock. A parrotfish blows a clear, jellylike bubble around itself when it wants to rest in the coral reef. The bubble protects the parrotfish from predators. (brown)

Some animals must borrow disguises or create hiding places from objects around them. The hermit crab lives in a hard shell left by another animal. Sea urchins cover themselves with rocks and seashells. (blue)

All animals find some way to protect themselves from their predators. Think about other animals you have seen that have special hiding places. (red)

In this particular think aloud, Brian was given all four paragraphs to consider, scrambled in the following way.

1. Blue: Some animals borrow disguises. . . .
2. Yellow: Most animals face the problem. . . .
3. Red: All animals find some way. . . .
4. Brown: A turtle tucks itself. . . .

Brian's think aloud is brief. After considering all four paragraphs, he said, "I don't know. It looks okay the way it is. It talks about how animals hide. The different ways. . . .I want to leave it . . .the way it is."

Brian's reluctance to manipulate the passage is, in part, a result of little direct instruction in text structure patterns. One collection of words and paragraphs is about as good as another in his view. How can you help students like Brian develop a sense of text structure?

The following section describes graphic and structural organizers, two strategies you may want to use to help students grasp an author's structure.

Graphic Organizers

A graphic organizer is a visual display of the hierarchical structure of ideas in a text (Earle & Barron, 1973). A partially completed, teacher constructed graphic organizer can help students become sensitive to an author's text structure (Readence, Bean, & Baldwin, 1985). First, identify the dominant structure of a text passage. For example, the following passage from a children's book, *How Come . . . ? Easy Answers to Hard Questions* (Richards & Perl, 1975, p. 20) answers the question, "How does a caterpillar become a butterfly?" It represents an informational pattern typical of expository text material students read in school.

> A caterpillar is a butterfly's baby and it grows in three stages: egg, caterpillar, chrysalis. The tiny egg is laid by its mother on a favorite leaf. Soon the tiny caterpillar inside chews through its shell and begins eating its leaf and every other leaf around. It is very greedy.
>
> It grows very fat, very fast. Its old skin gets too small and it has to wiggle out of it. A soft new skin is always ready underneath. This process is called molting. It molts four or five times in butterfly babyhood.
>
> Sometimes it changes color and spots after a molt. But it keeps six real legs and all its soft baby legs to support its long back.
>
> Then one day it loses its appetite and leaves its leaf. It goes looking up and down stems and stalks for a safe place to become a chrysalis. This will be its last molt. It gets a new skin and a new shape. It may look like a twig or a piece of bark. It stays quiet in its chrysalis for a long time.
>
> Then one morning — pop! — the chrysalis cracks. And a gorgeous butterfly pokes out. Its wings are wet and rumpled at first. But soon it dries out and flutters off into the sun to mate with another butterfly. More eggs, caterpillars, chrysalids. The cycle never stops.
>
> (Used by permission of publisher.)

This partially completed graphic organizer is designed to key students to the structure of the passage and the three stages of a caterpillar's transition to a butterfly.

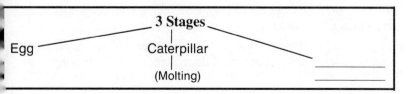

Students have to complete the graphic organizer by identifying the third and final stage leading to the formation of a butterfly. Subsequent informational passages then can be introduced to show their similarity and help students actively look for signal words such as "3 Stages" in the case of this passage.

McGee and Richgels (1985) recommend teaching elementary students about text structure patterns through writing activities. Students are given a graphic organizer like the one shown with all the slots filled and interrelationships of ideas shown before reading a passage. Before reading the passage, they are asked to write their own selection based on the information in the organizer. This student generated passage is then compared with the actual text. Students can see similarities and differences and eventually move toward more challenging activities including developing their own graphic organizers (Bean et al., 1986) or they can evaluate and rewrite ill structured passages (McGee & Richgels, 1985). Alvermann (1986) describes additional forms of graphic organizers that help students grasp a knowledge of text structure and a metacognitive strategy they can apply on their own.

Structural Organizers

Slater, Graves, and Piché (1985) developed a procedure called a structural organizer for explicitly introducing students to the structure of a text passage. Basically, a structural organizer consists of an explanation of why using an author's pattern of organization is important, alerting students to the actual pattern of organization they will encounter in a reading assignment and guiding their use of this pattern by supplying a partially completed outline of the text to be filled in as they read. Slater et al. found that ninth grade students' comprehension of social studies text was significantly better when a teacher used structural organizers students completed as opposed to teacher generated organizers and more traditional study strategies. These results were true for high, middle, and low ability students.

The following structural organizer was devised to accompany a newspaper article about the Hmong people who recently immigrated to the United States from Laos (Paterno, 1986). For the purposes of this illustration, only an adaption of an excerpt of the article will be used.

Problem Solution Structural Organizer

As you read this newspaper article, notice how the author organizes ideas into a problem solution structure. Doing this will help your understanding in at least three ways: The problem solution structure will help you remember more of what you are reading, you will be able to recall more of the major ideas (problems), and you should be able to remember this information for a longer period of time.

The article describes the problems confronting a group of people who must leave their homeland of Laos for the United States. As you read the article, look for the problems these people experience and think about solutions you might offer. The outline that follows has a place where you can write each of the problems. Do this as you are reading, not after reading. Each problem can be found by locating its paragraph number in parentheses ( ) on the outline and in the text.

A Quick Journey from the 16th Century to the 20th
Susan Paterno

1. Problem (paragraph 2)
   The Hmong expected Americans to greet them as heroes. Few Americans knew about the war in Laos or about the Hmong.

2. Problem (paragraph 4)
   _____

   _____

3. Problem (paragraph 6)
   _____

   _____

   Solution
   _____

   _____

4. Problem (paragraph 8)
   _____

   _____

Solution

_____

_____

5. Problem (paragraph 9)

_____

6. Problem (paragraph 10)

_____

Solution

_____

A Quick Journey from the 16 Century to the 20th
Susan Paterno

(1) After the war, thousands of the Hmong fled Laos to escape torture and death as the Pathet Lao army took over. They spent years in refugee camps before coming to the United States, to live in the cities where sponsors could be found.

(2) Most Hmong expected Americans to greet them as heroes, since thousands died fighting as U.S. allies. But few Americans knew about the war in Laos, and fewer knew or cared about the Hmong.

(3) Nai Her tried to practice his English with a young woman sitting next to him on a bus. She rebuked him. "Why are you here?" Why don't you go back to your own country? You're not working; you're all on welfare."

(4) Racism is only one of the Hmong's problems. When refugees come here, everything that was true is no longer. Americans tell refugees their values are wrong, and the refugees no longer know what is right.

(5) Many Hmong hoped to retain the traditions that kept their communities stable in Laos—arranged marriages, polygamy, patriarchy. As animists, they respect the spirits of the river, wind, sea, and sky. They honor ancestors in ceremonies that transport their spiritual leaders into the netherworld by way of convulsions and trances.

(6) Forced to abandon their culture in most U.S. cities, the Hmong began migrating, just as they had done in Laos

when their lifestyle was threatened. Many headed for California's central valley hoping to farm. 18,000 drifted to Fresno, Merced, and Stockton, following a path forged years earlier by the Basques, Armenians, Japanese, and Oklahoma's Dust Bowl victims.

(7) Most Hmong cannot find jobs; funds to support them are dwindling. Roughly 60 percent are unemployed (down from 90 percent a few years ago).

(8) When the Hmong arrived, Fresno school officials complained about Hmong children, who came to class with head lice and terrible odor. The children's families knew nothing about soap or toothpaste or changing clothes. According to Eileen Riley, a teacher who oversees the Fresno school district's migrant education program, "they'd sleep in their clothes and wear them day after day. We got them nightgowns and we taught them hygiene. They're very receptive."

(9) Hmong always wear clothes covering the area from their waist to their knees, even when alone. In the refugee camp, one Hmong woman asked about bathing in America. The woman was horrified at the description of taking a shower. "I could never take my clothes off," the woman said. "I'd be much too embarassed, even if I were alone." Even in the United States, Hmong women shower wearing sarongs; men wear shorts. Many teenage girls would rather drop out of school than shower after gym class.

(10) Another problem: Hmong girls were leaving seventh or eighth grade to get married. It's against U.S. law, but in their law, marriages are arranged and girls do what their parents tell them. However, that is changing fast; they realize the only way to succeed here is to become Americanized.

(11) Americanization has its painful aspects. Older Hmong worry that their adult children will send them to die in nursing homes. Meanwhile, Hmong teenagers fit in by forming rock bands, spiking their hair, and wearing heavy makeup.

Both graphic organizers and structural organizers help students develop foundational knowledge about a topic. This is an important first step in any lesson sequence but it is not enough. The article about the Hmong people implies that the solution to the Hmong's culture shock is to assimilate—to abandon their ways and Americanize. This unidimensional solution could be a springboard for a problem solving discussion in class that explores less ethnocentric solutions. Careful teacher questioning might elicit more creative, less culturally biased solutions from students. In essence, understanding an author's pattern of organization is a starting point, a foundation for creative, critical thinking.

Both graphic and structural organizers take teacher time to develop and introduce but their benefit to students makes the effort worthwhile. Both strategies prime students to pay attention to an author's use of language in an informed fashion.

Summary

In this chapter, research on text structure showed that teaching students to perceive an author's structural cues helps comprehension and recall of information. The value of observing students' use of these cues during the normal flow of classroom instruction was discussed, and think aloud protocol analysis was demonstrated as a means of observing individual students. Finally, two teaching strategies—graphic organizers and structural organizers—were introduced. Both are designed to enhance students' metacognitive awareness and use of text structure.

References

Alvermann, D.E. Graphic organizers: Cuing devices for comprehending and remembering main ideas. In J.F. Baumann (Ed.), *Teaching main idea comprehension*. Newark, DE: International Reading Association, 1986, 210-226.

Alvermann, D.E. Restructuring text facilitates written recall of main ideas. *Journal of Reading*, 1982, *25*, 754-758.

Bean, T.W., Singer, H., Sorter, J., and Frazee, C. The effect of metacognitive instruction in outlining and graphic organizer construction on students' comprehension in a tenth grade world history class. *Journal of Reading Behavior*, 1986, *18*, 153-169.

Christen, W.L., Searfoss, L.W., and Bean, T.W. *Improving communication through writing and reading*. Dubuque, IA: Kendall/Hunt, 1984.

Earle, R.A., and Barron, R.F. An approach for teaching vocabulary in content subjects. In H.L. Herber and R.F. Barron (Eds.), *Research in reading in the content areas: Second year report*. Syracuse, NY: Reading and Language Arts Center, Syracuse University, 1973, 84-110.

Bean

Glazer, S.M., and Searfoss, L.W. Reexamining reading diagnosis. In S.M. Glazer, L.W. Searfoss, and L.M. Gentile (Eds.), *Reexaming reading diagnosis: New trends and procedures.* Newark, DE: International Reading Association, 1988.

Graesser, A.C. *Prose comprehension beyond the word.* New York: Springer-Verlag, 1981.

Lipson, M.Y., and Wixson, K.K. Reading disability research: An interactionist perspective. *Review of Educational Research,* 1986, *56,* 111-136.

Lytle, S. *Exploring comprehension style: A study of twelfth grade readers' transactions with text.* Ann Arbor, MI: University Microfilm, 1982.

McCauley, J.R. *Animals and their hiding places.* Washington, DC: National Geographic Society, 1986.

McGee, L.M., and Richgels, D.J. Attending to text structure: A comprehension strategy. In E.K. Dishner, T.W. Bean, J.E. Readence, and D.W. Moore (Eds.), *Reading in the content areas: Improving classroom instruction,* second edition. Dubuque, IA: Kendall/Hunt, 1986.

McGee, L.M., and Richgels, D.J. Teaching expository text structure to elementary students. *The Reading Teacher,* 1985, *38,* 739-748.

Meyer, B.J.F., Brandt, D., and Bluth, G.J. Use of top level structure in text: Key for reading comprehension of ninth grade students. *Reading Research Quarterly,* 1980, *16,* 72-103.

Meyer, B.J.F., and Rice, E. The structure of text. In P.D. Pearson (Ed.), *Handbook of reading research.* New York. Longman, 1984, 319-351.

Moore, D.W. A case for naturalistic assessment of reading comprehension. In E.K. Dishner, T.W. Bean, J.E. Readence, and D.W. Moore (Eds.), *Reading in the content areas: Improving classroom instruction.* Dubuque, IA: Kendall/Hunt, 1986, 159-170.

Olshavsky, J. Reading as problem solving: An investigation of strategies. *Reading Research Quarterly,* 1977, *12,* 654-674.

Paterno. S. A quick journey from the 16th century to the 20th. *The Orange County Register,* August 1986, J-1.

Pearson, P.D., and Camperell, K. Comprehension of text structures. In H. Singer, and R.B. Ruddell (Eds.), *Theoretical models and processes of reading,* third edition. Newark, DE: International Reading Association, 1985, 323-342.

Readence, J.E., Bean, T.W., and Baldwin, R.S. *Reading in the content areas: An integrated approach,* second edition. Dubuque, IA: Kendall/Hunt, 1985.

Richards, J. Illustrated by S. Perl. *How come . . .? Easy answers to hard questions.* New York: Platt and Munk, 1975.

Richgels, D.J., McGee, L.M., Lomax, R.G., and Sheard, C. Awareness of four text structures: Effects on recall of expository test. *Reading Research Quarterly,* 1987, *22,* 177-196.

Rose, M. The language of exclusion: Writing instruction at the university. *College English,* 1985, *47,* 341-359.

Slater, W.H., Graves, M.F., and Piché, G.L. Effects of structural organizers on ninth grade students' comprehension and recall of four patterns of expository text. *Reading Research Quarterly,* 1985, *20,* 189-202.

Retelling Stories as a Diagnostic Tool

T his chapter describes retelling as a diagnostic tool for assessing comprehension of text and stories, sense of story structure, and language complexity. In addition, some consideration is given to retelling as an instructional strategy. Although retelling has been used as an assessment tool in research investigations, it is not widely recognized as a technique for diagnosis or measurement in the classroom. Similarly, it is not widely used as an instructional strategy, although investigations have demonstrated its ability to improve comprehension, sense of story structure, and language complexity (Morrow, 1985; Gambrell, Pfeiffer, & Wilson, 1985; Zimiles & Kuhns, 1976).

In story retelling, as the technique is discussed in this chapter, an individual recalls orally a text or story after having read or listened to it. As Johnston (1983, p. 54) points out, "Retelling is the most straightforward assessment . . . of the result of text-reader interaction." It is often used as an assessment tool in reading research. Because retelling can indicate a reader's or listener's assimilation and reconstruction of text information, it can reflect comprehension. It has at least one advantage over the more traditional practice of assessing comprehension through questions: Retelling allows a reader or listener to structure response according to personal and individual interpretations of the text.

Procedures for Eliciting Retellings

Retelling is not an easy procedure for students, no matter what their ages and especially if they have had no prior experience.

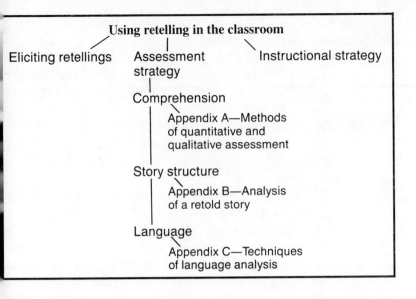

Morrow (1985) found that children had difficulty retelling, but practice added to the quality of retellings and to the ease with which students approached the task. Children need guidance and practice before retelling is used in formal evaluation of any of their skills or abilities.

Students should be told before reading or listening to a text or story that they will be asked to retell it. Further guidance depends on the purpose for retelling. If the immediate intent is to teach or test sequence, the child should be instructed to concentrate on what happened first, second, and so on. If the goal is to teach or assess ability to integrate information and make inferences from text, the child should be instructed to refer to personal feelings or experiences related to the text. Props such as feltboard story characters, graphs, or pictures from text can aid students in retelling. In using retelling as a teaching technique, pre and post discussions of the story or text will often help improve the skill of retelling (Mitchell, 1984; Morrow, 1985). It is also helpful to conduct followup practice sessions and discussions about the quality of retelling.

Because accurate assessment depends on accurate analysis, children's retelling should be recorded for playbacks as needed by the examiner or analyst. Guidelines for eliciting and coaching a child's retelling follow (Morrow, 1985):

1. Ask the child to retell the story by saying, "A little while ago, I read the story (name the story). Would you retell the story as if you were telling it to a friend who has never heard it before?"

2. Use the following prompts only when necessary:

    If the child has difficulty beginning the story retelling, suggest beginning with "Once upon a time. . ." or "Once there was. . . ."

    If the child stops retelling before the end of the story, encourage continuation by asking, "What comes next?" or "Then what happened?"

    If the child stops retelling and cannot continue with the prompts offered, ask a question about the story that is relevant at that point in the story at which the child has paused. For example, "What was Jenny's problem in the story?"

3. When a child is unable to retell the story, or if his or her retelling lacks sequence and detail, prompt the retelling step by step. For example:

    "Once upon a time. . . ," or "Once there was. . . ."

    "Who was the story about?"

    "When did the story happen?" (day, night, summer, winter)

    "Where did the story happen?"

    "What was the main character's problem in the story?"

    "How did she try to solve her problems?" "What did she do first/next?"

    "How was the problem solved?"

    "How did the story end?"

Retelling for Assessment

In retelling for purposes of evaluation, students should be told before reading or listening to a story that they will be asked to retell it. Depending on the information the evaluator is looking for, students also should be given a stated purpose for their reading/listening. If a specific skill is to be analyzed in the assessment, students should be advised to pay particular attention to that skill. For example, if the ability to sequence is to be assessed, the evaluator should tell students that in retelling the story they should try to tell it with events in the order in which they happened.

Unlike retelling for instructional purposes, retelling for assessment should be carried out without prompts, props, or use of text/story. The text/story should not be discussed with the child after reading/listening and before retelling. Simply ask the child to retell the story/text as if telling it to a friend who has never heard it before.

Retelling for Comprehension

Retelling offers the potential of measuring both the product and process of comprehension (Morrow et al., 1986). Children's ability for literal recall—remembering facts, details, cause and effect relationships, sequencing of events—can be diagnosed through retelling. Children reveal their ability to make inferences as they organize, integrate, and classify information that is implied but not expressed in the text story. In such instances, children may generalize, interpret feelings, relate ideas to their own experiences (Irwin & Mitchell, 1983; Lanier & Davis, 1972; McConaughy, 1980; Morrow, 1984), and engage in holistic comprehension (Morrow et al., 1986).

To assess comprehension through retellings, both quantitative and qualitative methods should be considered.

In quantitative assessment, readers or listeners should be directed to retell all they can remember from the text. The examiner will have parsed the story/text into units to be assessed (e.g., propositions, idea units, elements of story structure). The protocol of the reader's/listener's retelling is then parsed into identical units and compared with the text units. The match between protocol units and text units represents the reader's/listener's comprehension score (Gambrell, Pfeiffer, & Wilson, 1985; Kintsch & Kozimnsky, 1977; Morrow et al., 1986).

Quantitative assessment has both advantages and disadvantages in measuring comprehension. It tends to reflect recall of text based facts, details, sequence, and structural elements. On the other hand, it does not provide for scoring inferences that indicate links children make between text and prior experience. Usually it does not rate the importance of the various units of information recalled in the retelling. Mitchell (1985) notes that in determining comprehension, both quality and quantity of information are important.

Qualitative assessment focuses on children's deeper understanding of the story/text. Sometimes referred to as holistic ratings, qualitative analyses take into account student's generalizations beyond the text (e.g., interpretive remarks, ability to summarize, biases for or against information in the text). In addition to major points and details, qualitative assessment documents supplementation, coherence, completeness, and comprehensibility (Irwin & Mitchell, 1983).

Similar to the holistic grading systems for written composition developed by Cooper (1977) and Meyers (1980), qualitative analysis for retelling is based on the premise that the whole piece is more important than any of its parts and holds that a subject's total impression of a sample includes all those elements.

Appendix A offers samples of both quantitative and qualitative procedures for assessment of retelling.

Retelling Sense of Story Structure

Retelling makes it possible to assess the form of comprehension evident in children's sense of story structure. Mandler and Johnson (1977), Rumelhart (1975), Stein and Glenn (1979), and Thorndyke (1977) have described story structures and story grammars. According to these investigators, well formed stories have structures that include *setting* (time, place, characters), *theme* (an initiating event that causes the main character to react, form a goal, or face a problem), *plot episodes* (events in which main character attempts to attain goal or solve the problem), and a *resolution* (attainment of goal or solution of problem and ending of the story, which may have long term consequences).

While ages seem to determine the number of story elements children typically include in their retellings, several researchers have reported that young children generally have some concept of story structure (Applebee, 1978; Mandler & Johnson, 1977; Stein & Glenn, 1979; Thorndyke, 1977). From ages four to six, children tend to include settings, beginnings, and outcomes in their retellings. Early elementary students also include reactions, attempts, and endings. One researcher (McConaughy, 1980) found that younger children more easily recall story elements that contribute more directly to meaning.

Enhancing comprehension through development of a sense of story structure has become an area of greater interest among educators. In several studies children have been trained to develop awareness of story schemata by identifying and labeling structure elements within stories. Results indicate significant growth in comprehension (Bowman, 1981; Gordon & Braun, 1982; Spiegel & Whaley, 1980). On the other hand, children with little or no sense of story structure tend toward "fractured" retellings, with elements missing, unexplained, or out of sequence (Bower, 1976). If children are encouraged to develop and use schemata in retelling stories, they can anticipate elements of a story and decide which are most important to remember (McConaughy, 1980; Sadow, 1982; Whaley, 1981a). Whaley (1981b) reinforces the idea that children can develop a sense of story structure by retelling stories.

In summary, retelling can both develop and reveal children's sense of story structure. Assessment of retelling can identify the structural elements children include in a retelling and thus measure their sense of story structure.

To assess a child's retelling for its sense of story structure or inclusion of structural elements, the examiner should first parse the story into four scoreable units: setting, theme, plot episodes, and resolution. A fifth element, sequence, offers the opportunity to evaluate how appropriately the child retells the story in sequential order.

The child is then asked to retell the story. To analyze the retelling for its inclusion of structural elements, the examiner notes the number of idea units the child includes within the first four structural categories, regardless of order. A story guidesheet, outlining the parsed text, is used to record the idea units the child includes in the retelling. The child receives credit for a partial recall or for recounting the gist of a story element (Pellegrini & Galda, 1982; Thorndyke, 1977).

Having checked off the child's inclusion of elements, the examiner observes sequence by comparing or contrasting the order of elements in the child's retelling with the proper order of setting, theme, plot, episodes, resolution.

The analysis indicates the elements a child includes or omits, how well a child sequences, and where instruction might be necessary to develop an area in which the child's retelling has been particularly weak.

The procedure can be used with a point system that allows quantification of scores for an indication of a child's progress over a period of time. Appendix B illustrates analysis of a retold story with a parsed story, a sample verbatim transcription of a retold story, and a story retelling evaluation guidesheet with a sample analysis of a retelling.

Retelling for Measuring Language

In addition to offering a source of information for assessing comprehension and sense of story structure, retelling provides a corpus of uninterrupted language for assessment. The language sample generated during a retelling can be analyzed for number of words, number of different words, number of T-units, T-unit lengths, pronunciation, and syntactic complexity. Analysis of syntactic complexity reveals types of sentence patterns a child uses as well as grammatical structure. Knowledge and use of language is crucial to a child's development of literacy. Frequent analysis and assessment of samples of a child's oral language are desirable in guiding instruction. Retellings provide easily obtainable language samples for such assessment.

Developmental studies of oral language indicate that length of T-unit it is a reliable measure of language complexity (Hunt, 1965; Morrow, 1978; O'Donnell, Griffin, & Norris, 1967). Hunt describes the T-unit as an independent clause with all of its subordinate clauses attached. Thus, it may be equal to either a simple or a complex sentence. A compound sentence, however, is by definition made up of two or more T-units. To analyze a story or text retelling for T-units, transcribe the child's taped language and divide it into T-units. Record the number of T-units and the number of words for each. To find the average number of words, divide the total of words for all T-units by the total number of T-units.

For a more specific analysis of syntactic complexity, the Botel, Dawkins, and Granowsky (1972) formula (BDG) can be used. The formula is based on (1) transformational grammar theory, (2) language performance studies indicating the frequency with which children at various ages use various grammatical structures, and (3) experimental findings that indicate the relative difficulties children have in processing specific syntactic structures. As a tool for language analysis, the BDG formula identifies the elements of syntax and assigns each a weight of 0, 1, 2, or 3 to designate its relative difficulty. To determine the syntactic complexity of a language sample, count the total weights in each sentence in a group of sentences, then average the weights per sentence.

Appendix C illustrates these techniques of language analysis by providing a verbatim transcription of a retelling, its segmentation into T-units, and the BDG formula with an application of it.

Retelling as an Instructional Strategy

Research on verbal learning indicates that verbal rehearsal improves memory and recall for both children and adults (Craik & Watkins, 1973; Ornstein & Naus, 1978). In addition to its versatility as an assessment tool, retelling (a form of verbal rehearsal) has been demonstrated to be a valuable instructional strategy with either story or factual material.

Numerous benefits have been documented for reading to youngsters, then asking them to retell what they have heard. Such practice helps children develop sophisticated language structures, accumulate background information, and develop an interest in learning to read (Bower, 1976; Chomsky, 1972; Cohen, 1968; Durkin, 1966). Children's participation in literary experiences with adults aids and enhances their comprehension ability, oral language, and sense of story structure (Blank & Sheldon, 1971; Bower, 1976). Research results reported by Brown (1975) indicated that children's active involvement in reconstructing a story (thinking about events in a story, then arranging pictures of the story in sequence) facilitated their comprehension, apparently because in so doing they had internalized a representation of the story. Pellegrini and Galda (1982) found that children's comprehension of story and their ability to retell stories both improved with active involvement and peer interaction in story reconstruction through role playing. Further indications that retelling offers the child a large and active role in reconstructing stories and provides valuable interaction between teller and listener were reported by Amato and Ziegler (1973).

Even though it has not been widely tested, there is research evidence of retelling's potential in skill development. Further support for the notion appears in studies of strategies other than retelling that share some of its characteristics. For example, Blank and Sheldon (1971) measured semantic recall and syntactic complexity and found enhancement of both factors in four to six year olds who were asked to repeat sentences during a story reading. Zimiles and Kuhns (1976) found that retelling a story soon after it was read to them not only aided children in comprehension, but facilitated later recall. Three studies (Morrow, 1984, 1985, 1986) determined specific instructional benefits of story retelling among kindergartners. After listening to eight weekly stories and retelling them individually to research assistants, students in experimental groups improved significantly in oral language complexity, comprehension of story, sense of story structure, and inclusion of structural elements in dictations of original stories.

In spite of such evidence, children are rarely afforded the opportunity to retell stories in school. A survey of nursery school and kindergarten practice (Morrow, 1982) not only documented that fact, but found that teachers typically view retelling as time consuming and too difficult for children. In light of the research evidence of its educational value, those attitudes need to be reversed. Retelling should be encouraged with such supplemental techniques and materials as feltboards, role playing, story sharing among classmates, and puppets.

Because it engages the student in holistic comprehension and organization of thought, retelling of text acquired information is central to the suggestion that retelling enhances comprehension. It encourages both integration and personalization of content, helping the student see how parts of the text interrelate and how they mesh with one's own experience. As such, retelling follows a model of generative learning (Wittrock, 1981). Holistic in its approach, concept, and effect, retelling contrasts with the more traditional piecemeal approach of teacher posed questions that require students to respond with splinters of information recalled from text.

Research on retelling as a pedagogical tool for improving reading comprehension unsurprisingly is sparse, given the apparent adverse attitudes of most classroom teachers. Of the research carried out, Rose, Cundick and Higbee (1984) found that the reading comprehension of elementary school age learning disabled children was increased significantly by verbal rehearsal. The importance of that finding is all the more critical since Tarver, Hallahan, and Kauffman (1976) and Wong, Wong, and Foth (1977) found that reading deficits in learning disabled children are associated with deficiencies in developing mnemonic strategies. According to a study by Torgensen (1977), learning disabled children employ verbal rehearsal strategies less often than do normal elementary school readers.

Investigating the effects of retelling on the reading comprehension of fourth grade students, Gambrell, Pfeiffer, and Wilson (1985) found superior performance among students who engaged in retelling over four practice sessions when compared with students in the control group, who engaged simply in illustrating texts. Not only did their superior performance carry through on both immediate and delayed recall, but they correctly answered more literal and inferential questions about the test passage than did their counterparts in the control group. Results of the study suggest that (1) verbal rehearsal improves both comprehension and recall of discourse; and (2) through verbal rehearsal, the reader/listener learns something about the organization and retention of text information. Apparently, retelling, both during the processing of textual information (Rose, Cundick, & Higbee, 1984) and following it (Gambrell,

Pfeiffer, & Wilson, 1985), helps youngsters to plan, organize, and deploy their processing abilities more effectively.

Summary

Retelling is valuable for both assessment and instruction, and teachers should use it to assess a child's sense of story structure, comprehension, oral language complexity, and reproduction and production of stories and text. Analysis of a retelling can help a teacher identify problems not obvious when a student is asked simply to answer questions (Marshall, 1983).

Different retelling assessment strategies can be used to measure different skills, even though there are strengths and weaknesses in each. Variables such as memory, linguistic frequency, and task awareness can confound the results of retelling assessment. Teachers need to be aware of such weaknesses and strengths, even as researchers continue to develop still newer diagnostic measures to improvement retelling as an assessment tool (Mitchell, 1984).

Because retelling has the potential to improve and develop the same skills it can assess, it should be used for both purposes. Both as an instructional strategy and an assessment tool, retelling helps move teachers away from the view that reading is a set of isolated skills to a view of reading as a process for conveying and recreating meaning.

Appendix A
Quantitative and Qualitative Procedures
for Assessing Retelling

Quantitative: Evaluating Free Recall*

1. Divide the passage to be read into units of your own choosing — for instance, by phrases or clauses. Mark the end of each unit with a slash. Be consistent in your unit definitions and divisions from passage to passage.
2. On a sheet of paper, list your units in sequence, with empty lines to the left and to the right of each unit, forming three columns down the sheet.
3. Assign each unit a number from 1 to 3 and write the number in the blank to the left of each unit: 1 for an important unit like a main idea, 2 for a moderately important unit, and 3 for an unimportant detail.
4. Let the student read or listen to the story in its original format, then ask the student to retell it, using prompts as necessary.
5. Record the student's retelling on tape.
6. Analyze the student's recorded retelling by numbering the units on the right hand side of your guidesheet in the sequence in which the student has recalled them. Leave a blank by those units the student did not recall.
7. Compare the sequence in which the student has recalled the units with their sequence in the original story.
8. Tabulate the number of units the student recalled.
9. Note the assigned level of importance of each unit the student recalled.
10. To quantify the data, divide the number of recalled units at each level of importance by the total number of units at that level in the original story. The resulting three percentages indicate how closely the student's comprehension is biased toward the more important units.

---

* Adapted from Charles H. Clark, Assessing free recall. *The Reading Teacher*, 1982, *35*, 434-439.

*Qualitative: The Retelling Profile**

Directions. Indicate with a checkmark the extent to which the reader's retelling includes or provides evidence of the following information.

	none	low degree	moderate degree	high degree
1. Retelling includes information directly stated in text.				
2. Retelling includes information inferred directly or indirectly from text.				
3. Retelling includes what is important to remember from the text.				
4. Retelling provides relevant content and concepts.				
5. Retelling indicates reader's attempt to connect background knowledge to text information.				
6. Retelling indicates reader's attempt to make summary statements or generalizations based on text that can be applied to the real world.				
7. Retelling indicates highly individualistic and creative impressions of or reactions to the text.				

Morrow

	none	low degree	moderate degree	high degree
8. Retelling indicates the reader's affective involvement with the text.				
9. Retelling demonstrates appropriate use of language (vocabulary, sentence structure, language conventions).				
10. Retelling indicates reader's ability to organize or compose the retelling.				
11. Retelling demonstrates the reader's sense of audience or purpose.				
12. Retelling indicates the reader's control of the mechanics of speaking or writing.				

Interpretation. Items 1-4 indicate the reader's comprehension of textual information; items 5-8 indicate metacognitive awareness, strategy use, and involvement with text; items 9-12 indicate facility with language and language development.

* From P.A. Irwin and J.N. Mitchell. *The reader retelling profile: Using retellings to make instructional decisions,* in preparation.

Appendix B
Sample Analysis of Retelling

Parsed Story: Jenny Learns a Lesson

Setting

Once upon a time there was girl who liked to play pretend.
Characters: Jenny (main character), Nicholas, Sam, Mei Su, Shags the dog.

Theme

Every time Jenny played with her friends, she bossed them and insisted they do what she wanted them to.

Plot Episodes

First Episode. Jenny decided to pretend to be a queen. She called her friends and they came to play. Jenny told them all what to do and was bossy. The friends became angry and left.

Second Episode. Jenny decided to play dancer, with the same results as in the first episode.

Third Episode. Jenny decided to play pirate, again with the same results.

Fourth Episode. Jenny decided to play she was a duchess, again with the same results.

Fifth Episode. Jenny's friends decided not to play with her again because she was so bossy. Many days passed and Jenny became lonely. She went to her friends and apologized to them for being bossy.

Resolution

a. The friends all played together, with each person doing what he or she wanted to.
b. They all had a wonderful day and were so tired they fell asleep.

Once upon a time there's a girl named Jenny and she called her friends over and they played queen and went to the palace. They had to, they had to do what she said and they didn't like it, so they went home and said that was boring. . . . It's not fun playing queen and doing what she says you have to. So they didn't play with her for seven days and she had. . . she had an idea that she was being selfish, so she went to find her friends and said, I'm sorry I was so mean. And said, let's play pirate, and they played pirate and they went onto the ropes. Then they played that she was a fancy lady playing house. And they have tea. And they played what they wanted and they were happy . . . . The End.

Story Retelling Analysis

Child's name _____ Beth _____ Age ___ 5 _____

Title of story ___ Jenny Learns a Lesson ___ Date _____

General directions: Place a 1 next to each element if the child includes it in his or her presentation. Credit gist as well as obvious recall, counting *boy, girl,* or *dog,* for instance, under characters named, as well as *Nicholas, Mei Su,* or *Shags.* Credit plurals (*friends,* for instance) as two.

Sense of Story Structure

Setting

a. Begins story with an introduction   1

b. Names main character   1

c. Number of other characters named   2

d. Actual number of other characters   4

e. Score for other characters (c/d)   .5

f. Includes statement about time or place   1

Theme

Refers to main character's primary goal or problem to be solved   1

Plot Episodes

    a. Number of episodes recalled   4

    b. Number of episodes in story   5

    c. Score for plot episodes (a/b)   .8

Resolution

    a. Names problem solution/goal
        attainment   1

    b. Ends story   1

Sequence

Retells story in structural order: setting, theme, plot episodes, resolution. (Score 2 for proper, 1 for partial, 0 for no sequence evident   1

Highest score possible   10   Child's score   8.3

Morrow

Appendix C
Assessing Language Ability

Verbatim Transcription of a Retelling, Kevin, Age 5

Once upon a time a rabbit couldn't see. He went to play with his friends and he keeped on tripping and he keeped getting lost. He went to the doctor and he gave him glasses. Then he can see. When he played marbles he hitted a golden, red shiny one and the next day he played catch and he didn't even miss. He could help his mother go shopping. Now he was happy. He had glasses and could see.

Story Segmented into T-units

A T-unit is an independent clause with all of its subordinate clauses attached. It may be either simple or complex, but a compound sentence by definition is made up of two or more T-units.

		T-unit length
1.	Once upon a time a rabbit couldn't see.	8
2.	He went to play with his friends.	7
3.	And he keeped tripping.	4
4.	And he keeped getting lost.	5
5.	He went to the doctor.	5
6.	And he gave him glasses.	5
7.	Then he can see.	4
8.	When he played marbles he hitted a golden, red shiny one.	11
9.	And the next day he played catch.	7
10.	And he didn't even miss.	5
11.	He could help his mother go shopping now.	8
12.	He was happy.	3
13.	He had glasses and could see.	6

T-unit analysis

Total number of words	78
Total number of T-units	13
Average words per T-unit	6

Summary of BDG Syntactic Complexity Count

0-Count Structures	1-Count Structures	2-Count Structures	3-Count Structures

1. Sentence patterns
  a. subject-verb (adverb)
  b. subject-verb-adjective
  c. subject-*be*-complement (noun, adjective, adverb)
  d. subject-verb-infinitive
 	
2. Simple transformations
  a. interrogative
  b. exclamatory
  c. imperative
 	
3. Coordinate clauses joined by *and*
 	
4. Nonsentence expressions
	1. Sentence patterns
	  a. subject-verb-indirect object-object
	  b. subject-verb-object-complement
	
	2. Noun modifiers
	  a. adjectives
	  b. possessives
	  c. quantitative determiners
	  d. predeterminers
	  e. participle
	  f. prepositional phrase
	
	3. Other modifiers
	  a. adverbials
	  b. modals
	  c. negatives
	  d. set expressions
	  e. infinitives
	  f. gerund used as a subject
	
	4. Coordinates
	  a. coordinate clause joined by *but, for, so,* or *yet*
	  b. deletion in the coordinate clause
	  c. paired coordinates
		1. Passive
		
		2. Paired conjunction
		
		3. Dependent clause
		
		4. Comparatives
		
		5. Participles (not used in the adjective position)
		
		6. Infinitives as subjects
		
		7. Appositives
		
		8. Conjunction adverbs
			1. Clause used as a subject
			
			2. Absolute

From M. Botel, J. Dawkins, and A. Granowsky. *Syntactic complexity: Analyzing it and measuring it.* University of Pennsylvania, 1972.

BDG Worksheet

Child   (Kevin)   Age   (5)   Grade   (Kdg)   Sex   (Male)

T-Unit and Language Utterances	Sentence Length	0-Count Items	1-count Items	2-Count Items	3-Count Items	Total
Once…see	8	SVO	Set expression, negative			2
He…friends	7	SVO	Prepositional phrase			1
And…tripping	4	SVO				0
And…lost	5	SVO				0
He…doctor	5	SVO				0
And…glasses	5		SVIoO			1
Then…see	4	SVO				0
When…one	11		3 Adjectives	Dependent clause		3
And…catch	7	SVO	Adverbial begins sentence			1
And…miss	5	SVO	Negative adverb			2
He…now	8		Adverb SVOC			2
He…happy	3	SVO				0
He…see	6	SVO	Deletion in suborbinate clause			1

Total Count __13__

Average Complexity Count __1.00__

Average Sentence Length __6 words__

References

Amato, T., and Ziegler, E. The effectiveness of creative dynamics and storytelling in a library setting. *Journal of Educational Research*, 1973, *67*, 161-181.

Applebee, A.N. *A child's concept of story.* Chicago: University of Chicago Press, 1978.

Blank, M., and Sheldon, F. Story recall in kindergarten children: Effect of method of presentation on psycholinguistic performance. *Child Development*, 1971, *42*, 299-313.

Bower, G. Experiments on story understanding and recall. *The Quarterly Journal of Experimental Psychology*, 1976, *28*, 511-534.

Bowman, M. *The effects of story structure questioning upon reading comprehension.* Paper presented at the American Educational Research Association meeting, Los Angeles, California, April 1981.

Brown, A. Recognition, reconstruction, and recall of narrative sequences of preoperational children. *Child Development*, 1975, *46*, 155-166.

Chomsky, C. Write now, read later. *Childhood Education*, 1972, *47*, 296-299.

Cohen, D. The effect of literature on vocabulary and reading achievement. *Elementary English*, 1968, *45*, 209-213, 217.

Cooper, C.R. Holistic evaluation of writing. In Charles R. Cooper and Lee Odell (Eds.), *Evaluating writing: Describing, measuring, judging.* Urbana, IL: National Council of Teachers of English, 1977, 3-31.

Craik, F.I., and Watkins, M.J. The role of verbal rehearsal on short term memory. *Journal of Verbal Learning and Verbal Behavior*, 1973, *12*, 599-607.

Durkin, D. *Children who read early: Two longitudinal studies.* New York: Teachers College Press, 1966.

Gambrell, L., Pfeiffer, W., and Wilson, R. The effects of retelling upon reading comprehension and recall of text information. *Journal of Educational Research*, 1985, *78*, 216-220.

Gordon, C., and Braun, C. Story schemata: Metatextual aid to reading and writing. In J. Niles and L. Harris (Eds.), *New inquiries in reading and research and instruction*, thirty-first yearbook of the National Reading Conference. Rochester, NY: National Reading Conference, 1982, 262-268.

Hunt, K. *Grammatical structures written at three grade levels*, Report No. 3. Urbana, IL: National Council of Teachers of English, 1965.

Irwin, P.A., and Mitchell, J.N. A procedure for assessing the richness of retellings. *Journal of Reading*, 1983, *26*, 391-396.

Johnston, P.H. *Reading comprehension assessment: A cognitive basis.* Newark, DE: International Reading Association, 1983, 54-56.

Kintsch, W., and Kozimnsky, E. Summarizing stories after reading and listening. *Journal of Educational Psychology*, 1977, *69*, 491-499.

Lanier, R., and Davis, A. Developing comprehension through teacher made questions. *The Reading Teacher*, 1972, *26*, 153-157.

Mandler, J., and Johnson, M. Remembrance of things parsed: Story structures and recall. *Cognitive Psychology*, 1977, *9*, 111-151.

Marshall, N. Using story grammar to assess reading comprehension. *The Reading Teacher*, 1983, *36*, 616-620.

McConaughy, S. Using story structure in the classroom. *Language Arts*, 1980, *57*, 157-164.

Meyers, M. *A procedure for writing assessment and holistic scoring.* Urbana, IL: National Council of Teachers of English, 1980.

Mitchell, J.N. *Advantages and disadvantages of retelling for reading assessment.* Paper presented at the International Reading Association Convention, Atlanta, May 1984.

Mitchell, J.N. *Assessing written retellings of secondary students.* Paper presented at the National Reading Conference, San Diego, December 1985.

Morrow, L. Analysis of syntax, of six, seven, and eight year old children. *Research in the teaching of English*, 1978, *12*, 143-148.

Morrow, L. *Developing literacy early in life.* Englewood Cliffs, NJ: Prentice-Hall, in press.

Morrow, L. Effects of story retelling on young children's comprehension and sense of story structure. In J. Niles (Ed.), *Changing perspectives on research in reading/language processing and instruction,* Thirty-third yearbook of the National Reading Conference. Rochester, NY: National Reading Conference, 1984, 95-100.

Morrow, L. Effects of structural guidance in story retelling on children's dictation of original stories. *Journal of Reading Behavior,* 1986, *18,* 135-152.

Morrow, L. Relationships between literature programs, library corner designs, and children's use of literature. *Journal of Educational Research,* 1982, *75,* 339-344.

Morrow, L. Retelling stories: A strategy for improving young children's comprehension, concept of story structure, and oral language complexity. *Elementary School Journal,* 1985, *75,* 647-661.

Morrow, L., Gambrell, L., Kapinus, B., Koskinen, P., Marshall, N., and Mitchell, J. Retelling: A strategy for reading instruction and assessment. In J. Niles (Ed.), *Solving problems in literacy: Learners, teachers, and researchers,* Thirty-fifth yearbook of the National Reading Conference. Rochester, NY: National Reading Conference, 1986, 73-80.

O'Donnell, R., Griffin, J., and Norris, C. *Syntax of kindergarten and elementary school children: A transformational analysis,* Report No. 3. Urbana, IL: National Council of Teachers of English, 1967.

Ornstein, P.A., and Naus, M.J. Rehearsal processes in children's memory. In P.A. Ornstein (Ed.), *Memory development in children.* Hillsdale, NJ: Erlbaum, 1978, 69-99.

Pellegrini, A., and Galda, L. The effects of thematic fantasy play training on the development of children's story comprehension. *American Educational Research Journal,* 1982, *19,* 443-452.

Rose, M.C., Cundick, B.P., and Higbee, K.L. Verbal rehearsal and visual imagery: Mnemonic aids for learning disabled children. *Journal of Learning Disabilities,* 1984, *16,* 352-354.

Rumelhart, D. Notes on a schema for stories. In D. Bobrow and A. Collins (Eds.), *Representation and understanding: Studies in cognitive science.* New York: Academic Press, 1975, 211-236.

Sadow, M. The use of story grammar in the design of questions. *The Reading Teacher,* 1982, *35,* 518-521.

Spiegel, D., and Whaley, J. *Elevating comprehension skills by sensitizing students to structural aspects of narratives.* Paper presented at the National Reading Conference, San Diego, December 1980.

Stein, N., and Glenn, C. An analysis of study comprehension in elementary school children. In R. Freedle (Ed.), *New directions in discourse processes,* volume 2. Norwood, NJ: Ablex, 1979.

Tarver, S.G., Hallahan, D.P., and Kauffman, J.M. Verbal rehearsal and selective attention in children with learning disabilities: A developmental lag. *Journal of Experimental Child Psychology,* 1976, *22,* 375-385.

Thorndyke, R. Cognitive structures in comprehension and memory of narrative discourse. *Cognitive Psychology,* 1977, *9,* 77-110.

Torgesen, J.K. The role of nonspecific factors in the task performance of learning disabled children. *Child Development,* 1977, *48,* 56-60.

Whaley, J. Reader's expectations for story structure. *Reading Research Quarterly,* 1981a, *17,* 90-114.

Whaley, J. Story grammars and reading instruction. *The Reading Teacher,* 1981b, *34,* 762-771.

Wittrock, M.C. Reading comprehension. In F.J. Pirozzolo and M.D. Wittrock (Eds.), *Neuropsychological and cognitive processes in reading.* New York: Academic Press, 1981, 229-259.

Wong, B., Wong, R., and Foth, D. Recall and clustering of verbal materials among normal and poor readers. *Bulletin of the Psychonomic Society,* 1977, *10,* 375-378.

Zimiles, H., and Kuhns, M. *A developmental study of the retention of narrative material.* Washington, DC: National Institute of Education, 1976. (ED 160 978)

10 Albert J. Shannon

Using the Microcomputer Environment for Reading Diagnosis

I n the late 1970s, reading and language arts educators confronted new Information Age technology in the form of microcomputers. At first, teachers taught students *about* microcomputers. Now they are teaching students *how to use* microcomputers, and microcomputers have begun to play an important role in teaching and diagnosing students.

While classroom reading teachers, diagnosticians, and reading specialists have used microcomputers to supplement instruction, the role of technology in the diagnosis of reading disability remains comparatively new. As we reexamine and rethink diagnosis in this chapter, we will examine the potential and existing capabilities of the microcomputer in assisting the diagnostic process. Our goals are to explore the role the microcomputer can play in a whole language diagnostic setting and to explore the ultimate (future) potential of the microcomputer in the diagnosis of reading and language disability. It should be noted that this chapter presupposes a working knowledge of the microcomputer and of the types of software available for reading and language arts classes.

Diagnosis in the Whole Language Setting

In a diagnostic setting the microcomputer must be viewed as something different from the traditional "tool, tutor, tutee" paradigm. As we examine the relationship of students' reading, writing, speaking, and listening abilities, it is essential to view the micro-

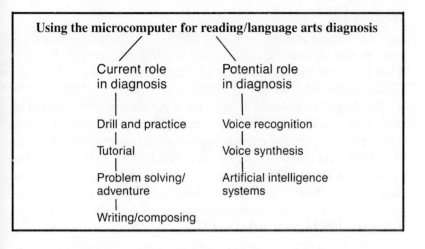

Using the microcomputer for reading/language arts diagnosis

Current role in diagnosis

Drill and practice

Tutorial

Problem solving/ adventure

Writing/composing

Potential role in diagnosis

Voice recognition

Voice synthesis

Artificial intelligence systems

computer as a specialized classroom/clinic microenvironment. In effect, the microcomputer creates a language environment in which the diagnostic process (described in earlier chapters) can take place. Students interacting with the microcomputer create a new setting for the exchange of ideas, experiences, feelings, emotions, and concepts. The interaction of students with a microcomputer provides opportunities for conversation, composition, experimentation, problem solving, adventure, simulation, and learning. Since the environment has become such an integral part of classrooms and clinics, reading professionals must capitalize on this opportunity for observing and recording language behaviors.

The reading and language related microcomputer environment allows students to engage in four language generating activities: drill and practice, tutorial, adventure/simulation and problem solving, and composing/writing. Each of these environments provides opportunities to diagnose students' language fluency, composing abilities, expression of self-concept, view of the world, and story sense. Each of these aspects is viewed as an important area of concern for reading diagnosis according to the model presented. My goal will be to define these settings, to offer practical guidelines for the observation and recording of language behaviors in these settings, and to provide instructional suggestions based on the diagnosis of language behaviors in these environments.

The Drill and Practice Environment

Drill and practice software follows the stimulus/reinforcement model of learning. While not intended to instruct, it is intended to reinforce and imprint previously taught skills. Its basic format is the continuous presentation of exercises (drills), often workbook style, requiring student input before the next question is presented. Student responses are reinforced (positively or negatively depending on the appropriateness of the answer), and records of success and failure kept. The software can be modified by the teacher to allow for control of speed, content, length of lesson, and mastery level. The nature of the software requires that one student at a time interact with the microcomputer; small homogeneous groups also might be effective in this setting.

Since student interaction with the microcomputer's software offers insight into reading and language behaviors, reading professionals are encouraged to record students' behaviors while using drill and practice software. The Observational Checklist for Students Using Drill and Practice Software offers some guidelines.

Ethnographic Observation. Teachers must be cautious about overgeneralizing conclusions about ability or disability in reading based on a single observation. Diagnosticians are encouraged to continually observe student groupings in different settings before drawing conclusions. Observations often lead to further questions that, again, must be answered only after repeated, careful observation periods. Some practical interpretation of the observations has been included to assist the diagnostician. Further interpretation with additional data is recommended. The use of this and other checklists presented in this chapter are intended as only one piece of data in a full case study report.

Observations 1, 2, 3. Motivated readers have a greater chance for success than do nonmotivated readers. Positive rankings (scores = 5, 4) are one clear indication that reluctance toward reading likely will not be a cause of disability. Lower scores (0, 1, 2) indicate a potential problem with motivation.

Observation 4. The observation of a positive self-concept toward the reading process informs the diagnostician that this poten-

Observational Checklist for Students Using Drill and Practice Software

Observations	Yes					No
1. The student demonstrates a desire to find the correct response.	5	4	3	2	1	0
2. The student will freely choose to use the software again.	5	4	3	2	1	0
3. Rewards for correct answers assist the student to respond.	5	4	3	2	1	0
4. The student approaches the new software with confidence and no apparent fears.	5	4	3	2	1	0
5. The student can predict a computer generated consequence to a response.	5	4	3	2	1	0
6. The student realizes that selected commands cause the computer to respond.	5	4	3	2	1	0
7. The student becomes more successful with longer use of the software.	5	4	3	2	1	0
8. The student recognizes repeated language patterns in the exercises.	5	4	3	2	1	0
9. The student can reproduce the language pattern of the computer software exercises.	5	4	3	2	1	0
10. Other observations _____						

ially damaging roadblock is not contributing to disability. Any score below 3 is cause to explore self-concept as a potential etiology of disability.

Observations 5, 6, 7. The student's ability to predict and control the software gives the diagnostician baseline data on the student's reading comprehension. Positive observations (scores = 5, 4) show that student mastery of the content or skill presentation of the software is taking place; lower recorded observations indicate the opposite.

Observation 8, 9. Students' ability to recognize and reproduce language patterns is essential and often is prerequisite to efficient reading behavior. Teachers who can document students' understanding of language patterns realize that a lack of language fluency may not accompany the reading disability. Students who are unable to recognize repeated language patterns in reading demonstrate a lack of readiness for more complex syntactical patterns in text.

Tips on Using Drill and Practice Software

1. Drill and practice software is not intended to teach students. Use it only when you can expect at least a 75 percent success rate. Nothing will ruin computer interest, self-concept, and self-confidence more than a computer exercise that is too difficult for the learner.

2. Drill and practice software can be highly motivational for reluctant students. Occasionally allow it to replace less attractive workbook sessions. A motivated student using the computer may read more material at a high level than one exposed only to traditional workbooks.

3. Drill and practice software quickly becomes tiresome and boring for students. Allow 15-25 minutes of use daily. Ideally the teacher should observe students by using the suggested checklist in the middle period of use.

4. If the drill and practice software is modifiable, make sure the content, speed, reinforcement, and pace are adjusted for each student. Diagnosis using the checklist would yield unreliable data if the reading level of the software was not suited to the student.

5. Keep records of student performance on the software to adjust future instruction. Continual diagnosis is best.

6. Coordinate the drill and practice software content with your curriculum in reading and language arts. Give students opportunity for practice in areas covered in recent lessons.

7. Do not use drill and practice software as a reward or punishment for completed/noncompleted, required work. Allow all students equal access, depending on their needs.

8. Demonstrate cooperative use of the microcomputer if your resources are limited. Students can benefit from small group drill and practice software; observe language interaction in these settings.

9. Choose drill and practice software that encourages language use

Shannon

and thought; mindless key pushing will not produce desired results.

10. Select drill and practice software that randomizes practice sessions for students. Repetitive programs do not benefit the learner.

11. Choose drill and practice software with an internal diagnostic branch that automatically moves to questions at an appropriate level based on user input.

The Tutorial Environment

Tutorial software typically follows a Presentation-Practice-Apply-Evaluate model of learning. Textual or graphic information is presented to the student; the student is given an opportunity to re-state the information or complete practice exercises with the new data. If the new information is understood, the student applies the information in a microcomputer generated activity to imprint the knowledge. Tutorials typically conclude with an evaluation of the user's understanding of the concepts presented in a set of straightforward questions testing the information. A criterion test score often is presented upon completion of the evaluation.

Sophisticated tutorial software often employs leveled branches that adjust the difficulty and subsequent teaching based on the student's previous answers to evaluation questions in the software. Subject matter of tutorials is as broad as the field of reading and language arts. Vocabulary, comprehension, study skills, phonics, grammar, writing, and punctuation have all been adapted to the tutorial software format.

While the nature of the software typically requires participation by only one student, small group work is easily accomplished by using the microcomputer as a visual teaching aid for the group. The software often keeps records of student performance that can be used for continued placement and diagnosis.

Since student interaction with the microcomputer's tutorial software offers insight into reading and language behaviors, reading professionals are encouraged to record the behaviors of students engaged in learning with tutorial software. The Checklist for Students Using Tutorial Software provides guidelines.

Checklist for Students Using Tutorial Software

Observations	Responses					
	Yes					No
1. The student demonstrates a desire to learn from the microcomputer.	5	4	3	2	1	0
2. The student remembers new information presented in the software (short term).	5	4	3	2	1	0
3. The student can remember information for the short term, but not for the long term.	5	4	3	2	1	0
4. The student uses aids (notes, returning to the text) to assist comprehension.	5	4	3	2	1	0
5. The student uses memory/study techniques to assist comprehension (SQ3R, ReQuest, mnemonic devices).	5	4	3	2	1	0
6. The student requires the information to be presented more than once for understanding.	5	4	3	2	1	0
7. The student continually recycles through the tutorial stages of the software (unable to master the concepts).	5	4	3	2	1	0
8. The student becomes frustrated with the software.	5	4	3	2	1	0
9. The student connects new information presented in the software with past knowledge or experience.	5	4	3	2	1	0
10. Other observations _____						

Observation 1. Motivated readers have a greater chance for success than do reluctant readers. Reluctance to use the reading software should not be confused with disability.

Observations 2, 3, 4, 5. The method students use to remember information can be observed and evaluated when students interact with tutorial software. Unobtrusive observation will indicate memory techniques the student uses. Special notes on how the student studies or remembers will serve the diagnostic process.

Observations 6, 7, 8. Metacognitive strategies can be observed by using these guidelines. If the student consistently elects to stop, regress, and reread information, teachers will realize that comprehension monitoring is not simultaneous with the reading act (as it should be). Students who consistently recycle through information for comprehension should be identified for remediation in this area. A high positive (scores = 4, 5) observation for question 8 should be scrutinized. A high score is clear indication that the reading level of the tutorial is beyond the student's capabilities.

Observation 9. A student's ability to connect new information with old indicates sophisticated reading behavior. Lack of adequate background should be made known to the diagnostician early in the attempted reading. Identifying a lack of background information as the etiology of comprehension disability is a precise diagnosis that should not be confounded with more recognizable reading comprehension deficiencies.

Tips on Using Tutorial Software

1. Do not use tutorial software to replace introductory teaching of a new concept. Make sure students have some background in the topic before they use software.
2. Tutorial software should be on the student's independent reading level to ensure focus on content rather than on the reading process.
3. Tutorial software should automatically branch to easier material when the student enters two or three wrong answers. Avoid frustration.
4. Tutorial software should use periodic, randomized reinforcement incentives for students. There is no need to shoot stars and ring bells for every correct response.
5. Tutorial software should set realistic mastery goals for the student and consistently report learning progress throughout the work session.
6. Content of tutorial software should be coordinated with your curriculum in reading and language arts. Students should be given an opportunity for independent work in areas covered in recent lessons.
7. Do not use tutorial software as a reward or punishment for completed/noncompleted, required work. It might effectively be used for make up or independent work. Allow all students equal access, depending on their needs.
8. Demonstrate cooperative use of the microcomputer if your resources are limited. Students can benefit from small group tutorial software; observe language interaction in these settings.

9. Choose tutorial software that encourages language use, notetaking, writing, or discussion away from the computer. Encourage students to discuss their experiences in other classroom settings.

The Problem Solving/Adventure Environment

Problem solving and adventure software use more of the capabilities of the microcomputer than any other type of instructional software. This software includes simulation, gaming, problem solving, interactive fiction, adventure, and creative art types of programs.

As its name implies, problem solving software asks students to solve a problem in logical thinking. The variety of software includes mystery stories, brain teaser puzzles, deductive reasoning problems, and simulations. A dominant genre in this area of microcomputer software is the interactive fiction story, where the student reader becomes a character in the story with the ability to control the plot.

Essential elements in the problem solving software are based on probabilistic and deterministic models. Programs based on probabilistic models randomly challenge the user to overcome difficulty, solve a dilemma, or complete a task. Those based on the deterministic model base all computer responses to the user on the previous problem solving decisions and input by the user (i.e., no random or chance occurrences). The more deterministic the model, the more closely the problem solving behavior approaches the type of thinking involved in real life.

Creative art programs simply use the microcomputer as an artistic medium. Divergent thinking is encouraged, and the student uses the microcomputer to diagram ideas, paint scenes, create designs, or produce animated pictures on the screen. Most programs allow the use of color, permit the saving of art work, and the modification of an on disk library. Art created with these software packages often acts as a precursor to writing or is later added to student's writing composition.

Since student interaction with the microcomputer's problem solving/adventure software offers insight into reading and language behaviors, reading professionals are encouraged to record the be-

Observational Checklist for Students Using
Problem Solving/Adventure Software

Observations	Responses					
	Yes					No
1. The student continues to use a problem solving strategy that has been successful in the past.	5	4	3	2	1	0
2. The student attempts to manipulate the problem/adventure story to his/her advantage.	5	4	3	2	1	0
3. The student attempts to organize the information presented in the problem for later recall.	5	4	3	2	1	0
4. The student can predict solutions to the problem based on information in the software.	5	4	3	2	1	0
5. The student can relate relevant personal background experiences to the software.	5	4	3	2	1	0
6. The student can follow the directions/hints given by the software.	5	4	3	2	1	0
7. The student realizes that a complex problem can be divided into subparts.	5	4	3	2	1	0
8. The student realizes that subparts can be put together to form a whole.	5	4	3	2	1	0
9. The student realizes that there is a beginning, middle, and end to the problem (story sense).	5	4	3	2	1	0
10. Other observations _____						

haviors of students learning with this software. Examine the Observational Checklist for Students Using Problem Solving/Adventure Software for guidelines.

Observations 1, 2. A student's ability to capitalize on and repeat successful behavior is essential for reading. If a student can solve a problem and repeat that problem solving behavior, the chance is minimized that initial success was random. Establishing control over an environment develops the self-confidence requisite to successful reading. Students who achieve success by chance, not by plan, will feel no control over text in reading.

Observations 3, 4. Organization and prediction abilities are requisite for reading comprehension. Observing a successful organizer will give the diagnostician background information vital for correct diagnosis. Knowing that a student can predict offers insight into a student's comprehension abilities. Positive observational rankings in these two areas (scores = 4, 5) indicate the student is using appropriate metacognitive strategies that will lead to comprehension.

Observation 5. If the student has relevant background experiences in the topic, the potential is enhanced for text comprehension. Students realizing similarities between reading and previous experiences are in an advantageous position.

Observation 6. Comprehending directions in software programs is essential for success. Diagnosticians observing students completing software without outside help can be assured students have some ability to read for following directions. Negative rankings on the observations in this area (scores = 2, 1, 0) indicate the software is above the reading level of the student user.

Observations 7, 8, 9. Students with sophisticated cognitive schemata will realize that most often the whole is the sum of the parts. They will perceive sequence and summation in a problem or a story. Deficient abilities in these areas would cause grave concern to the diagnostician observing a student in the microcomputer environment. Students lacking in conceptual, organizational, or story sense abilities will suffer severely in reading comprehension related activities.

Tips on Using Problem Solving/Adventure Software
1. Problem solving/adventure software is used most successfully in small groups. Since students will be using language and verbalizing problem solving strategies, the verbal and thinking interaction between students and microcomputer is best observed when two to four students use the software in a group.
2. Integrating problem solving software into the curriculum is a particular challenge. A match is needed between the type of thinking required at a particular stage in the curriculum and the type of thinking taught in the software. The focus in the match should be on the thinking required.
3. Adventure software supplements the literature curriculum. While

Shannon

not typically classified as reading software, this literature is as close a parallel to traditional book reading as the computer can provide. Adventure software should be used in the language arts program in the same manner as books are used in the classroom.

4. Problem solving software is not an end in itself. The skills and abilities reinforced or learned in this experience must be transferred by the student (with the aid of the teacher) to the language arts area of the curriculum. Once a problem has been solved using a particular line of reasoning, the teacher must provide an example of using the skill in the subject being taught.

5. Demonstrate cooperative use of the microcomputer if your resources are limited. Students can benefit from small group problem solving, interactive fiction, and adventure software. Observe language interaction in these settings.

6. Choose software that encourages language use, notetaking, writing, and discussion away from the computer. Encourage students to discuss their solutions to problems, experiences with adventures or simulations with peers in other classroom settings.

7. Encourage the use of the creative art software in conjunction with your creative writing program. Computer generated graphics add prestige and expertise to student work and often serve as prewriting stimuli.

8. Gaming software is easily modifiable to include concepts from the language arts curriculum. Since playing a game to reach a goal (or be the winner) involves strategies similar to problem solving, encourage cooperation in the use of this type of software.

Diagnosis in the Writing/Composing Environment

Word processing software and computer assisted writing programs are two types of programs students typically use in the composing process. Educators agree that word and text processing are the most commonly used types of software in elementary and secondary schools.

In effect, word processing programs turn the microcomputer into an electronic typewriter allowing on screen correction of errors, multiple editing tasks, and disk storage of writing. Word processing programs are available at all levels of sophistication. Some programs allow complex margin setting, italicized writing, boldface printing, file merging, and page numbering; more simplified versions allow large screen printing, editing, and simple text moving procedures. Word processing software is logically viewed as a tool in the writing process.

Computer assisted writing, on the other hand, actually aids in the writing process. This type of software might assist students in any step of writing from the prewriting and drafting stages through revising, editing, and publishing the composition. There is software in this category designed to enhance the prewriting stages of the composition process by leading students through the brainstorming and preorganizational steps of writing. There are templates or writing frames that allow students to fill in existing paragraph outlines with personalized information (i.e., the cloze procedure for creative writing) that assists students in revising their writing. Spelling and grammar checkers are designed to assist students in the editing and publication steps of writing by highlighting misspelled words, unacceptable punctuation, or incorrect grammatical formations. Paragraph, poetry, book report, and essay "frames" require students to insert key words to create the entire composition. Disk storage systems are available to save early drafts, count words, and calculate average sentence length. While all of these forms of assistance are potential aids in the writing process, teachers should note that abuse or overuse of the aids will not produce independent writers. The Observation Checklist for Students Using Writing/Composing Software provides some guidelines.

Observations 1, 2. The microcomputer environment is usually a motivating factor in the writing and revising process. The promise of using the microcomputer for composing often will motivate even the most reluctant of writers. Students with poor handwriting or self-expression skills often find the word processor to be the great equalizer. Since students typically spend more time composing and sharing when a microcomputer is available, diagnosticians should be aware of the power of the technology to influence both composing ability and time on task. Positive rankings in these observations (scores = 5, 4) would indicate the powerful effect of the microcomputer on the composing process.

Observation Checklist for Students Using Writing/Composing Software

Observations	Yes					No
	Responses					
1. The student has willingly chosen to write.	5 4 3 2 1 0					
2. The student takes pride in the finished product.	5 4 3 2 1 0					
3. The student has organized thoughts before approaching the microcomputer to write.	5 4 3 2 1 0					
4. The student composes from notes or prepared outlines.	5 4 3 2 1 0					
5. The student, when asked, can write based on personal experiences.	5 4 3 2 1 0					
6. The student's writing reflects some perception of how the student views reality.	5 4 3 2 1 0					
7. The student's writing reflects language patterns encountered in reading and speaking.	5 4 3 2 1 0					
8. The student uses editing and revision techniques to enhance writing.	5 4 3 2 1 0					
9. The student uses varied sentence structure and length in the composition.	5 4 3 2 1 0					
10. Other observations _____						

Observations 3, 4. Observing a student's preparedness to write is essential in the diagnosis of writing behavior. Students who begin the writing process at the drafting stage, ignoring the prewriting step, are clearly doomed to inadequate composition. Diagnosticians can easily identify a student who comes to the drafting stage, at the microcomputer, with writer's block; the student will have no notes, outline, or prepared ideas. Diagnosticians also have the opportunity to record and interpret student's prewriting rituals that may lead to success or failure in the composing process.

Observations 5, 6. Students' writing is most successful when based on personal experience and personal perceptions of the world. As the student is writing, the teacher can monitor the progression of words on the screen. (Standing behind students using computers allows the diagnostician to watch several writers at once.) The observing diagnostician has the opportunity to encourage the reluctant, suggest word revisions to the editors, and provide in text suggestions to those revising. This participatory observation also can be done with students in small group settings. While diagnostic observation in this setting is beneficial, leading questions geared to individual students provide instruction in writing ability as the student composes.

Observation 7. Beginning writing style often reflects the style of an author previously read by the students. A student who begins the writing process by imitating the style of another author demonstrates a sophisticated understanding of the patterning of text. Diagnosticians should capitalize on this ability by encouraging students to go beyond the imitated style to develop their own writing and language patterns.

Observations 8, 9. Teachers observing the writing behaviors of students must know if the current work is a first draft, a revision, or a final copy for publication. Student writing must be judged using different criteria in varying stages of development. Students who do not revise their writing, change text, or rework sentences are typically not as successful in the writing process as those who do. The microcomputer environment allows the diagnostician another opportunity to observe students of various stages of writing. Using observations similar to items 8 and 9 will provide deeper insight into the mental processes of students engaged in writing.

Tips on Using Writing/Composing Software
1. Adequate time must be provided for keyboarding/word processing instruction. While typing 8-12 words per minute is adequate for elementary composing, a period of time (20 minutes, 3 times per week) in the language arts curriculum must be committed to the task. Teaching writing must be integrated with instruction in the use of word processing.
2. Students should become familiar with word processing in small group, language experience activities directed by the teacher. A teacher, aide, or experienced student should be employed to assist inexperienced typists.
3. The keyboard should not replace the pen and pencil as composing instruments. Prewriting and organizing using conventional writing approaches can be done before arriving at the computer.

4. Teachers must reach a delicate balance between interfering in the writing process as they observe students compose and assisting the writing process cooperatively. Teachers should never take over the keyboard to control the writing of a student.
5. If possible, students who are prepared should be given open access to the microcomputer to begin the composing process. Prewriting and organization take varied amounts of time depending on the students. Using the word processor before the writer is ready will not produce the desired results.
6. Teach students the *replace* command of the word processing software early in the microcomputer training. The versatility and revision capabilities of this command will prove to be among the most satisfying for the student.
7. Demonstrate cooperative use of the microcomputer if your resources are limited. Students can benefit from small group writing and composing activities. The use of the language experience approach with small groups is an ideal use of the word processing software. Observe language interaction in these settings.
8. Encourage the use of the creative art software in conjunction with the creative writing program. Selected word processing software incorporates drawing or graphics programs. Story book creation programs exist to initiate the building of student authored libraries on disk.
9. Consistent use of the word processing software will ensure the continuous development of student expertise with the microcomputer. Alternative input devices (touch screens, modified keyboards) are available for handicapped students.

Potential Role of the Microcomputer in Reading Diagnosis

Using the microcomputer as a tool for the diagnosis of reading and language behaviors of students remains in its developmental stages. Software that purports to write a prescription based on a computer generated diagnostic reading test taken by the student is at best weak and overgeneralized and at worst misleading and inaccurate. There is, however, great potential for more fully developed software of this type to play a significant role in the diagnosis of reading and language behaviors in the 1990s.

The potential use of the microcomputer as a diagnostic tool (a role quite different from the microcomputer environment described to this point in the chapter) is dependent on the continued development of two areas of microcomputer technology: voice recognition/ voice synthesis and artificial intelligence. In short, for the microcomputer to be an effective tool for the diagnostician it must be able to listen to and speak to the reader via natural language transmissions, and it must be able to evaluate language behaviors and relevant testing data with the expertise of an appropriately trained reading professional.

Voice Recognition

Voice recognition is the ability of the microcomputer to understand the verbal input of the user. The limited capabilities of the microcomputer allow the speaker/user to use a limited vocabulary (up to 1,000 words with selected software) to interact with the microcomputer. Capabilities of the microcomputer to recognize voices require a "voice print" of each user. The procedure requires up to thirty minutes of interaction with the software before true use begins. Current voice recognition technology is reported as only 95 percent accurate, even after the voice print has been established. It is clear that a 5 percent error rate in listening to a reader's output is unacceptable for accurate reading/language diagnosis.

Voice Synthesis

Voice synthesis is the ability of the microcomputer to reproduce human sounding speech. Current technology has almost eliminated robotic, mechanical sounding speech, but it is far from a multitonal and inflectionally accurate reproduction of speech. Again, while some software is capable of reproducing up to 5,000 words, it is far from the accurate interactive speech necessary for reading or language diagnosis.

Artificial Intelligence Systems

Artificial intelligence systems (dubbed expert systems) appear as more sophisticated possibilities for the diagnosis of reading and language related behaviors. Expert systems are intelligent programs that output prescriptions based on data introduced by the user or specialist. Expert systems in use by the medical profession are able to diagnose selected diseases with up to 75 percent accuracy, when compared with the diagnosis of a trained physician. Comparable systems for the diagnosis of reading and language behaviors do not yet exist. The potential is excellent for an expert system to diagnose reading behaviors.

There are many problems associated with expert systems in the area of reading diagnosis. Expert systems are based on professionally agreed upon definitions and an accepted model of behavior or performance easily described and capable of precise delineation (e.g., symptoms of a medical disease). Herein lies the problem. When dealing with the cognitive and affective domains, precision is difficult to achieve. Furthermore, whose model of reading instruction would be employed by the expert systems? Would it be a sub-skills approach? A whole language model? A pure psycholinguistic approach? A combination? If an expert system diagnosed a vocabulary problem, would it recommend instruction in phonics, phrase reading, morphology, spelling, wide reading, or context clues? Would it be programed to diagnose specific phonological, semantic, or syntactic problems? Would comprehension instruction have priority over word recognition instruction? Is it possible to develop an expert system on a topic where there is substantial professional disagreement? The answers remain unknown, as does the future applicability of any expert system developed by a team of artificial intelligence experts, computer scientists, and reading professionals.

The potential is bright for using the microcomputer as a diagnostic tool, but there are significant problems. Reading professionals are cautioned to examine closely any software that claims diagnostic capabilities. The underlying concern that the software defines reading and language behavior in a way that is philosophically compatible to the user's definition is of vital importance. Concomitant concerns of how the program makes decisions, what alternative prescriptions are within its capabilities, and its ability to discriminate reading difficulties should be of highest concern to all reading professionals.

Summary

The microcomputer environment is an information laden setting to be explored by the reading teacher/diagnostician. Observations of students interacting with the dynamic print of microcomputer software can add valuable information to the total diagnosis of reading and language ability. This information – used in conjunction with information gathered in other settings, at other times, and under other conditions – will add significant diagnostic insight to a case report conducted by a reading professional.

Shannon

Physical Arrangements, Grouping, and Ethnographic Notetaking

T his chapter describes a classroom organized so that a teacher, reading specialist, or anyone involved in the diagnosis of a student's reading or learning problems will be able to observe the student effectively. This observer will use a structured, systematic method of note taking and record keeping to provide ongoing and constantly corrected diagnostic and prescriptive decisions about the student's performance.

Settings

How can school environments be arranged to provide teachers, diagnosticians, planners, and evaluators with opportunities to observe children's reading and other language abilities? School environments that best provide diagnostic information about children include the classroom (and specific areas in it), playground, lunchroom, gym, music room, art room, and even the school bus. Observers of children's language behavior – reading, speaking, listening, and hearing – can use any of the above environments to collect data about an individual, a small group, or a classroom of children.

Usually teachers/specialists who are engaged in diagnostic evaluation (as well as the planning that should follow such evaluation) have information available to them. This material is often the result of previous testing in a school office. This data may be called

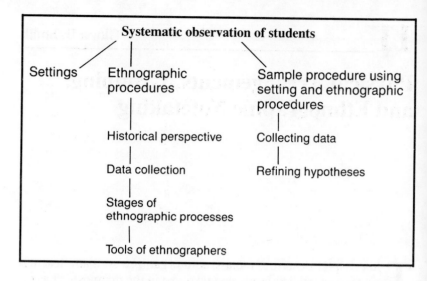

Systematic observation of students

Settings — Ethnographic procedures — Sample procedure using setting and ethnographic procedures

Historical perspective — Collecting data

Data collection — Refining hypotheses

Stages of ethnographic processes

Tools of ethnographers

the medical model material. It provides test scores and descriptions that usually were gathered during testing sessions with a specialist on the school staff. While this information is useful, teachers need to add to it by observing children. This chapter will help teachers use an information gathering system in a classroom to augment, supplement, and improve the information provided by the medical model. The C-A-L-M approach by Glazer and Searfoss, described in detail earlier in this monograph, is partly the basis for the material in this chapter.

An ideal setting for this diagnosis is a flexible classroom where desks can be moved, chairs of varying sizes are available, and the furniture is sturdy (Moffett & Wagner, 1976). There are fixed areas in the classroom, such as a library corner that has a rug and some seating pillows. This area has many books on numerous subjects and at varying levels of difficulty. There also is an art section in the classroom stocked with paper, paints, and crayons. An area is available where computers and their software are housed. In addition, there are cabinets for tape recorders and videocassettes. Teacher created learning centers are located around the room. There is nothing new about this kind of classroom; it is the ideal set up

(Sawada, 1986). What is new is the opportunity this setting provides for gathering and recording information to diagnose children's reading abilities and refine educational prescriptions for them.

Ethnographic Procedures

This system of recording observed behaviors is called ethnography. It is defined by Taylor (1982) as a "disciplined way of looking, asking, recording, reflecting, comparing, and reporting." Anthropologists have used it for many years but only recently have educators turned their attention to it (Pearson, 1984). Carini (1975) provides an in depth analysis of theory as well as a psychological description of interactions between the observer and the observed when observation and description of behavior are combined to produce ethnographic recordings.

Several studies have exemplified the use of ethnographic procedures as a way to record behavior. One such investigation (Bussis et al., 1986) provided research data on beginning reading. Twenty-six children were studied for two years (kindergarten through first grade) as the authors investigated and documented beginning reading processes and learning styles. Another study concentrated on the education of binational migrant children as they moved between Mexico and California (Mounts, 1986). A study conducted to examine differences in oral and written discourse in early grades (Slaughter et al., 1985) also describes a coding system for analysis of protocol data. Such examples suggest that educational research is widening its scope and using tools such as ethnography to diagnose, to refine diagnoses, and to prescribe appropriate educational programs for students.

Data Collection

For the purpose of this chapter, ethnography may be defined as a system of taking repeated and *detailed* notes about a subject or subjects in a single environment, for a specified time. Generations of well trained teachers have made detailed observations by taking informal notes. The reader is justified in asking, "So what's new?" The newness of the process concerns the last step: creating a hypothesis from the data collected. This fits the C-A-L-M approach with its insistence that data constantly be refined and new hypotheses created.

Ethnographic data may be collected by taking detailed, specific, and continuous notes for a specific time. These notes may be supplemented by using a videocamera to record behavior, or a tape recorder for voices. These devices tend to be intrusive and should be in place for several days before the actual data collecting begins so the subjects will not "play to the camera."

As the data accumulate, the observer should analyze the material and create new and refined hypotheses to narrow the focus of the data collecting. In other words, the researcher generates interpretations and "fine grained analyses" (Taylor, 1982). These interpretations produce new hypotheses. The data collection continues and the hypotheses are constantly changed as the observer gains new insights. As an analogy, the medical model is a photograph that freezes a person's behavior and accomplishments in time. The ethnographic or C-A-L-M approach may be compared to videotaping a persons' behavior and achievements over time.

Stages of Ethnographic Processes

Ethnographic approaches to reading research are investigated in detail by Guthrie and Hall (1984). They use Spindler's work (1982), which sets forth three stages of the ethnographic process. The first is *reconnaissance,* in which the ethnographer becomes familiar with the setting.

Second is the *reconnoiter* stage, where the observer begins to delineate the broader aspects of the investigation and examines general aspects of the environment. Analyses of behaviors are made as the data are collected. Then the first hypotheses are formed, tested, and accepted or refined, so data collecting may begin anew with a different focus. As is evident from these descriptions, ethnographic recordings tend to be cyclical.

The final stage is termed *microethnography.* In this phase, small pieces of human behavior are examined in detail. The teacher or researcher has some general knowledge of the student from previous ethnographic research and now takes one relevant aspect of behavior (e.g., reading silently during uninterrupted silent reading period) and makes detailed notes during the specific activity and period of time. This final stage refines the process so it is of use to teachers and researchers. At this stage, it may be possible to synthesize many observations and notes. The creation of useful, specific hypotheses will help form a useful teaching strategy.

Tools of Ethnographers

Ethnographers are either nonparticipating observers or participating observers as teachers would be (Spradley, 1980). In their participant observational studies, Walker and Adelman (1976) note that shared information must be understood in a context of long term shared meanings. Such information may be delivered by student or teacher by as little as a single phrase or key word. This stimulus word, which participants recognize from a previous experience, colors the present situation. It is important that observers be aware of classroom interactions so they may understand the observable behavior as well as the hidden messages being passed. Observers must remain objective and record all behavior of the subject(s) during the time chosen for the study.

Researchers may use one or all of several interviewing techniques (Spradley, 1979). They may use the structured interview to elicit information from people who interact with the child being studied, including parents, teachers, and after school daycare staff. Semistructured interviews also may be used. In these, the researcher has a set of questions to ask, but is willing to discard them if a promising lead is provided by the interviewee.

The researcher may also use a *key informant*. This person is interviewed to provide information about the subject, but the researcher also "discusses the research and checks out the hypotheses and hunches with him or her" (Pearson, 1984).

Journal entries and diaries may be of great use in ethnographic research. When children keep daily diaries, their entries may reveal how they feel about events in their lives and about their achievements in the classroom. It is important for those studying students to understand the children's beliefs, their feelings, and how they react to their failures and successes.

Sample Procedure Using Setting and Ethnographic Procedures

The teacher who has organized the ideal classroom described in the beginning of this article probably also has a class in which lecturing or "talking at" students is kept to a minimum. This teacher will have lesson plans and contracts for the children to encourage them to work independently and in self-directed groups. During these activities, the teacher (diagnostician, specialist) will establish a time for observation and taking notes on one child. A teacher who wishes to study a reluctant reader during Uninterrupted Sustained Silent Reading (USSR) might decide to begin an ethnographic record of this child's activities.

> 1:00 p.m. USSR—John removed book from desk—looked at cover—glanced at Fred—shifted in seat—leaned forward and whispered to Fred—(no reply)—settled back, opened book—turned pages—subvocalized as he read first page. . . .
> 1:06 J poked Fred—F turned and frowned—J looked at teacher—opened book and again started to read. . . .

The teacher might take notes during the USSR period for several weeks or for only two or three days. At the end of a period, the notes might be analyzed:

Analysis. John is not able to concentrate on his book during USSR.

John would like to socialize with Fred.

Then these hypotheses might be created.

1. John does not like to read silently in the book he has selected.
2. John is unable to read and comprehend the book he has selected.
3. John has strong needs to socialize.
4. John has a dependent relationship with Fred.

The teacher may test one of these hypotheses by taking notes about John in a classroom situation that will give more information. The first hypothesis may be examined by looking at records of John's reading scores (the medical model test results). His abilities may be discussed with a teacher who taught him the previous year or with the reading specialist who has known John since he began school. Either of these people might function as key informant for the studies. Informal reading tests might be given to John (Potter & Rae, 1973) to ascertain the level at which he reads. Or John might be instructed in the "fistful of words rule" (Glazer, 1980) so he will choose a book more appropriate to his reading level. There will be continued observation of how John acts in USSR.

In order to test the second hypothesis, the teacher could ask John to retell the story he has read (Morrow, 1986). The teacher might have John tape record his retelling so an analysis could be made of it. This will help to assess whether John has read and comprehended his book.

The teacher may choose to test the third and fourth hypotheses by taking notes about John when he is at recess or in the lunchroom, in order to have data that will help understand John's need to interact with other students. The teacher can observe him in situations where socializing is appropriate to see if John plays only with Fred, or if he plays with other children. Then reassessment can be made of his behavior in USSR and other silent reading sessions with more information available.

After establishing this new set of data, the teacher may decide to focus on John's behavior in other environments where he reads silently, such as a Directed Reading Activity. Does the additional data collected match that collected during USSR? What analysis and hypothesis does this set of notes provide? What other environment may be checked to verify or disprove the theories generated?

It should be apparent from the about discussion (which is greatly oversimplified for the sake of brevity) that John's teacher has a structured method of collecting data about him in an environment that makes such collecting possible. There is direct, sequential evidence provided by observations of John's behavior during this one time period. Other sources to supplement this information may be used: teacher observations of John during the school day; and John's school records, school tests, and reports of school personnel ranging from the playground aide to the principal. This information will give a more complete picture of the subject. The canvas will never be a finished product, but, rather, one that is changed and made more faithful to its subject. Thus, the picture of John will change as environments change, and diagnosis and remediation will probably become more accurate.

The perceptive teacher may also use John's journal entries to gather information about his feelings toward reading in any form. When this writing/reading activity is used, pupils are told that only the teacher will read their journals. The teacher responds to what students write every day, but does not correct grammar, punctuation, or handwriting. Teacher responses to pupils' entries should be as positive as possible. As students learn to trust the teacher, a wealth of material may be collected about students' feelings and attitudes. Such knowledge must be kept confidential in order to have the children continue to trust the teacher. However, this material will also help diagnose John's attitudes and ideas about reading.

The teacher is able to use this system of ethnographic recording because the classroom setting encourages children to act independently; it is child centered (Moffett & Wagner, 1976) and uses the student's self-motivation to provide an impetus for learning. While children move about in a classroom that has a strict, underlying structure, but which allows them appropriate freedom, the teacher may have periods of time to make notes on the student being diagnosed.

Obviously, teachers will not take ethnographic notes on each student. They will choose the one who is a puzzle, or who is unmotivated, or one for whom ordinary strategies do not work. Then, by this intense system, they may be able to diagnose and prescribe to the benefit of the student. They will have a powerful set of tools to help them become the excellent teachers they wish to be.

Summary

This extended method of diagnosis may be called the educational model of diagnosis; it retains the medical model, and it is implemented by the Glazer-Searfoss c-a-l-m approach. It takes place in a classroom that can be changed and reorganized easily; it insists on structured, detailed, specific observations for a limited time and in a specific environment. It is never ending. It is constantly revised. It is open ended. No one specialist, diagnostician, teacher, or evaluator presumes to know everything about a student. (See Abrams, this volume.) Those who work with students revise their evaluations periodically and prescribe educational strategies and techniques for them. As students mature, the diagnosis must change, and as the diagnosis changes, new strategies must be suggested. In the beginning of this chapter, the medical model was described as a snapsphot of a child—a picture frozen in time. The educational model provides pictures of children in many activities as they change and mature.

References

Bussis, A.M., Chittenden, E.A., Amarel, M., and Klausner, E. *Inquiry into meaning: An investigation of learning to read.* Hillsdale, NJ: Erlbaum, 1985.

Carini, P.F. *Observation and description: An alternative methodology for the investigation of human phenomena.* Grand Forks, ND: University of North Dakota, 1975.

Carini, P.F. *The school lives of seven children: A five year study.* Grand Forks, ND: University of North Dakota, 1975.

Glazer, S.M., and Searfoss, L.W. *Reading diagnosis and instruction: A C-A-L-M approach.* Englewood Cliffs, NJ: Prentice-Hall, 1988.

Glazer, S.M. *Getting ready to read: Creating readers from birth through six.* Englewood Cliffs, NJ: Prentice-Hall, 1980.

Guthrie, L.F., and Hall, W.S. Ethnographic approaches to reading research. In P.D. Pearson (Ed.), *Handbook of reading research.* New York: Longman, 1984.

Moffett, J., and Wagner, B.J. *Student-centered language arts and reading, K-13: A handbook for teachers.* Boston: Houghton Mifflin, 1976.

Morrow, L.M. *Retelling stories and text: A diagnostic tool.* Paper presented at the International Reading Association Eleventh World Congress, London, July 1986.

Mounts, D.D. *The binational migrant child: A research project.* Sacramento, CA: California State Department of Education, 1986.

Potter, T.C., and Rae, G. *Informal reading diagnosis.* Englewood Cliffs, NJ: Prentice-Hall, 1973.

Pearson, P. David (Ed.). *Handbook of reading research.* New York: Longman, 1984.

Sawada, D. Spontaneous creativity in the classroom. *Humanistic Education and Development,* 1986, *25,* 2-12.

Slaughter, H.B., and Others. *Contextual differences in oral and written discourse during early literacy instruction.* Paper presented at the annual meeting of the American Educational Research Association, Chicago, April 1985.

Spindler, G. (Ed.). *Doing the ethnography of schooling: Educational anthropology in action.* New York: Holt, Rinehart & Winston, 1982.

Spradley, J.P. *The ethnographic interview.* New York: Holt, Rinehart & Winston, 1979.

Spradley, J.P. *Participant observation.* New York: Holt, Rinehart & Winston, 1980.

Taylor, D. *Working notes on ethnography.* Paper presented at Rider College Workshop, 1982.

Walker, R., and Adelman, C. Strawberries. In M. Stubbs and S. Delamount (Eds.), *Exploration in classroom observations.* New York: John Wiley and Sons, 1976.

Afterword

T he ideas and suggestions in this monograph not only help classroom teachers reexamine issues related to reading diagnosis but provide a rich and broader perspective of students' reading. The text is a valuable resource that aids teachers in their quest to identify students' reading strengths and weaknesses. The work is meant to encourage teachers to expand their view of reading measurement, to go beyond standardized test results in order to provide students with ongoing, meaningful assessment and instruction.

Historically, the use of standardized tests to evaluate reading performance has helped classify students in respect to word recognition, vocabulary, comprehension, and rate. However, many of these tests do not properly reflect the educational aims being sought. The focus on individual differences within or among groups in reading is limiting. It furnishes data for those interested in making broad comparisons of classrooms, schools, or school districts but provides little information to help teachers develop students' reading strengths and design instruction to advance their learning.

The trends of a rapidly changing American society require schools and teachers to broaden diagnosis and instruction in reading to meet the needs of multicultural students and socioeconomically diverse groups. We feel this monograph affords professionals at all levels innovative diagnostic tools and procedures necessary to help students adjust to reading and learning in today's classrooms.

SMG
LWS
LMG